BREAKING FREE FROM A NARCISSISTIC CO-PARENT

A COMPREHENSIVE GUIDE TO CO-PARENTING WITH A NARCISSISTIC EX, OVERCOMING THEIR CONTROL AND PROTECTING YOUR CHILDREN

MICHAEL MARINO

Lighthouse
BOOKS

First published in 2023 by Lighthouse Books LLC

contact@lighthousebooks.co

Disclaimer

This book is not intended as a substitute for professional, psychological, legal, or medical advice. Every situation is unique, and readers should consult with a qualified professional for their specific needs. The author and publisher disclaim any liability arising directly or indirectly from the use of this book.

CONTENTS

INTRODUCTION

Remember the beginning of *The Wizard of Oz*? Glinda, the Good Witch of the North, is standing there in her huge gown with her magic wand, and she tells Dorothy that she can't magic her back home. Instead, she points her toward the start of the Yellow Brick Road (Fleming, 1939).

Well, as much as I would like to magic all your co-parenting problems away, I'm afraid I can't. Nonetheless, this book will help you to start off on your journey. It will be a long journey, and you will no doubt have to battle lions, tigers, bears, and witches along the way. But just as Dorothy eventually discovered she had always had the power to get home, I hope this book will help you find the power that is within you to create the life you really desire for yourself and your family.

This book was created for those of you who found yourselves co-parenting with an ex-partner who may display narcissistic behavior or may be affected by Narcissistic Personality Disorder. It was designed to guide you on your co-parenting journey, which may be high-conflict and stressful, based on my professional experience and personal empathy for your situation. Although the guidelines discussed in this book may be often supported by scholarly research, I tried to maintain a conversational tone to avoid overwhelming you with academic publications and jargon and, instead, focus on conveying information plainly and in a nonjudgmental way.

As a professional psychologist, I have worked with numerous parents facing similar situations to yours. I have had the opportunity to engage in in-depth conversations regarding their concerns for their children. Combining this with years of extensive research into human psychology, I've been able to help countless families implement successful strategies for managing the issues of narcissistic, abusive, or uncooperative exes.

Besides my professional background, I understand the difficulties associated with breakups, mainly when an ex-partner exhibits traits of narcissism, having experienced challenging relationships with toxic individuals myself. I empathize with the sense of loss and confusion that often follows such an experience.

Furthermore, as a child of divorced parents, I understand the impact of divorce on children and that separating parents may sometimes introduce toxic family dynamics to children. Growing up, I was victimized by my parents' game-playing and manipulation, and this affected every aspect of my life. This made me committed to ensuring your children do not suffer a similar fate.

My parents' constant fighting led me to become a "people pleaser"—I was always trying to avoid conflict, so I defaulted to ensuring that my friends, colleagues, and partners were always happy. Never mind what I wanted or needed. I never felt like I mattered.

Fortunately, I worked to overcome my challenges and learnt how to form successful, happy relationships. Although it may be possible to move on from toxic relationships without any help, I would like to support you through this experience with the years of expertise I gained as a professional psychologist. I want you to know your children will be OK. They have you.

And you have support and guidance.

Over the last five years, I have spoken to many single parents. Most of them started off by asking me things like, "How did I manage to screw things up to this extent?" "Why am I such a failure?" And, "Why could I not have married a sweetheart and had a normal, idyllic family like everyone else?" It is so easy to fall down a rabbit hole of negative thoughts. But if you don't pull yourself out of that hole (and soon), you are going to fall deeper and deeper, and it will get harder and harder to climb out.

So I will tell you what I told them.

Firstly, it is essential to recognize that you are not a failure at all. Everybody makes decisions that don't turn out as they had hoped. But you noticed that something needed to change, and you took corrective action. That is not failure. That is strength. You care deeply about your children, and your willingness to seek help and guidance from this book is a testament to your dedication as a parent. You bought this book to help you move forward and address the issues you face. Again, none of that looks much like failure to me.

Secondly, it is essential to remember there is no such thing as a *normal* family—despite what you may see on social media or reality TV. Take what your sister says about her family with a pinch of salt and remember that your friend with her nuclear family has his own struggles behind closed doors. So your family may not fit the ideal image in your mind, but it can still be amazing, and it is yours.

I have no doubt that you begin this book with a great many questions. They may include the following:

- Is my ex actually a narcissist?
- How can I co-parent with someone like that?
- How can I create (and maintain) boundaries with my ex?
- What can I do if they are being totally unreasonable?
- How will it affect my children?
- What can I do to protect them?
- How do I look after myself in all this?
- Where do I begin?

I am here to help you answer those questions in this book. Together we will break down what co-parenting with a narcissist looks like and how you can take back control and make the most of the situation. By the end of the book, you will have a clear idea about your situation's challenges and how best to handle them.

CHAPTER 1
SO YOU'RE RAISING A CHILD WITH A NARCISSIST

Let's start by taking a close look at your situation because it's essential to clearly understand what you're up against. You know your ex is difficult and uncooperative, but are they actually a narcissist? You may be wondering what's going on in their head? How will this affect co-parenting? And how are you going to stay sane throughout all of this?

There are many questions, but don't worry, you will see some answers here. Further on in the chapter, you'll take the first step in preparing to deal with your ex-partner by learning strategies for building resilience and taking care of yourself. In the spirit of that, put your phone away, make yourself a coffee, and take the time you need to digest everything fully.

IS YOUR EX ACTUALLY A NARCISSIST

Narcissism is a term that's thrown around quite a bit. Some people may be called narcissists if they're arrogant or full of themselves. But what does the term mean?

Narcissism is named after the Greek myth of Narcissus. There are various versions of the myth, but in all of them, Narcissus is a handsome hunter who looks into a pool of water and falls in love with his own reflection. In some iterations, he kills himself because his love is not reciprocated. In others, he cannot leave the pool of water (and stop looking at himself), so eventually, he withers and dies. In the end, his excessive self-love leads to his downfall. Little wonder then that Narcissus gave his name to the psychological term "narcissism," which means excessive love of oneself.

Narcissism is not a black-and-white issue. It is a complex trait that exists on a spectrum. Some people exhibit healthy amounts of narcissism. Some have excessive narcissistic traits that lead to negative consequences. And some have Narcissistic Personality Disorder (or NPD for short), which is a mental health condition characterized by an exaggerated sense of self-importance.

It is important to note that everybody has some degree of narcissism, and this trait is particularly pronounced in children before the age of around eight. During this developmental stage, they may be very self-centered and prone to expressing anger and frustration when they don't get their way. Their sense of self-importance may be high, and a five-year-old may be usually not shy about displaying their talents, like drawing, running, or singing with pride. It is only later that they start to compare themselves to others and appreciate that they might not actually be better or more important than everyone else.

Hopefully, as individuals mature, they hang on to some "healthy narcissism," which, after all, is essential for maintaining a positive self-image and healthy relationships with others. This level involves having a healthy regard for one's own needs and importance. It enables individuals to have confidence, foster self-belief, and set healthy boundaries. Healthy narcissism, balanced with other opposing positive traits such as empathy, compassion, and humility, is essential for overall well-being. Otherwise, excessive narcissism can have negative consequences, leading to egocentrism, arrogance, and a lack of empathy for others.

At the extreme end of the narcissism spectrum is NPD, which is not a mere behavioral flaw; it's a serious mental health condition, classified as a personality disorder, that requires a professional diagnosis. People with NPD may exhibit a more extreme and dysfunctional form of narcissism. They have an inescapable pattern of grandiosity, a constant need for admiration, and a lack of empathy for others. This pattern of behavior and attitudes causes significant impairment in their personal, social, and occupational functioning. *The Diagnostic and Statistical Manual of Mental Disorders* (DSM) lists nine behavioral patterns used for diagnosing NPD (American Psychiatric Association, 2013):

- An overinflated sense of self-importance.
- Continuous thoughts about being more powerful, loved, successful, smart, attractive, and influential than others.
- Feeling superior and unique and only wanting to associate with others perceived as special or high-status people or institutions.

- The need for excessive admiration.
- A sense of entitlement.
- A willingness to exploit or take advantage of others to achieve goals.
- A lack of empathy.
- An envy of others or a belief that others are envious of them.
- Demonstrating arrogant and haughty behaviors and attitudes.

For a person to be diagnosed with NPD, they must meet five or more of these criteria according to DSM. But bear in mind—only a qualified mental health professional is equipped to make such a diagnosis. People can display one or more of these traits at different times without having NPD. It becomes a disorder when these traits persist and cause significant functional impairment or distress.

NPD is uncommon—experts estimate only 1–6% of the population is affected by it. But, as we've said, narcissism is on a spectrum. Individuals with narcissistic traits may exhibit some of the same behaviors and attitudes as someone with NPD but to a lesser degree and without the same level of dysfunction.

So what does this behavior look like

If these nine criteria are the ingredients of the narcissism cake, what does that cake actually look and taste like? How do narcissists typically behave?

Think about your ex. Do the statements below apply to them? Answer yes or no to each of these statements.

- They believe everyone is jealous of them.

- They were incredibly charming when you first met them.
- They often acted differently in public than they did at home.
- They always hogged the conversation and made everything about them.
- They always needed me to tell them how great they were.
- They were always big-upping their achievements and talents.
- They often criticized or looked down on others.
- They expected me to do what they wanted and got upset if I didn't.
- They always insisted on having the best of everything—cars, clothes, etc.
- They got angry quite easily.
- They would withdraw from or avoid situations where they might fail or someone else might be better than them.
- They were really competitive and hated losing.
- They made out like everything was a competition.
- They took advantage of others to get what they wanted.
- They acted impatient/bored/disinterested when I talked about my feelings or achievements.
- They didn't seem to care about my needs and put themselves first.
- They were super sensitive to criticism and were very easily slighted.
- They never apologized.
- They often put me down, belittled me, or made jokes intended to cause harm to me instead of being humorous.

- They didn't have many long-term friends.
- They often lied or tried to change things to suit their narrative.
- They would distort the meaning of previous conversations or incidents and make me second-guess myself.
- I felt more anxious and less confident around them.
- I often felt like everything I did was wrong.
- I used to apologize a lot.
- I commonly made excuses to others for their behavior.
- I often stopped myself from telling them about my achievements—as I knew this would upset them or they would put me down.

I suspect you answered yes to quite a lot of these. If so, it doesn't necessarily mean that your ex has NPD, but it does put them quite firmly on the narcissist spectrum.

The locked box

The really interesting thing about narcissists is that it's all a front. They are often quite damaged and vulnerable individuals who carry deep wounds from childhood experiences. They may present a persona of superiority because it allows them to shut their vulnerability away in a little box they don't have to open, which would expose their feelings of inferiority, emptiness, and shame. The severity of their inner turmoil drives them to avoid criticism, never admit fault, or acknowledge anyone's superiority, as it would mean exposing their innermost fears and insecurities. For this reason, they may strive to appear as if they can't be wrong, they can't be criticized, or they can't be made to feel like others are better than they are because that means opening that little box and facing what is inside.

If you have ended a relationship with a narcissist, you have taken an important step towards prioritizing your well-being. It is crucial to recognize that they may be deeply affected by the breakup. By forcing them to confront the contents of that locked box, potential consequences, such as abusive or defensive behavior, may result as they attempt to regain control.

CO-PARENTING WITH A NARCISSIST

So, we've concluded that your ex is a narcissist. What does that mean for your future in co-parenting? Well, you are most likely to face numerous challenges since co-parenting takes place when divorced parents have a mutual interest in their children's development and well-being. They can collaborate over important issues as well as the day-to-day logistics of having to bring up children in separate homes. They have decided to put the needs of the children above their own and can civilly and fairly divide their time and money to make sure their children have the support they need. Reasonable co-parents can put aside their own differences in the presence of their children. They can attend important functions and parent consultations together and take steps to ensure their children are not exposed to conflicts. This ability to prioritize their children's needs and well-being over their emotions is critical for successful co-parenting.

You can already see the problems here, right?

This whole co-parenting arrangement requires two people who understand fairness and put children's needs ahead of their own. As you've seen, narcissists are generally not skilled at either. When dealing with a narcissistic ex-partner, this level of maturity and cooperation may be impossible to achieve, as their focus might predominate on themselves and their own needs rather than those of the children.

Added to that, you are dealing with an emotionally vulnerable individual—your ex-partner's diminished ego may make things more difficult. While rejection can be painful for anyone, narcissists might react in ways that are abusive or defensive, using various tactics to regain control and restore their sense of superiority. Therefore, it is essential to approach the situation with caution to protect yourself and your children's well-being.

Issues that might arise

So, what kind of behaviors can you expect when co-parenting with a narcissist? Here are some examples of the problematic behaviors described on a regular basis by those co-parenting with narcissists. Perhaps you've experienced some of them already.

Co-parenting authority issues

- **Being argumentative**—They may argue in front of the children with the intent of causing chaos. For example, Susan's ex, Mark, would often wait until the children were present before engaging in heated arguments, making their children feel anxious and torn between their parents.
- **Undermining authority**—They may undermine your authority by allowing the children to break your rules, making it difficult for you to maintain consistency. For example, when their children were with Robert's ex-wife, Lisa, she would say that their father's rules were stupid and that they did not have to obey them.

- **Being stubborn and inflexible**—They may often display stubbornness and inflexibility, making co-parenting difficult. For example, Samantha struggled to co-parent with her ex, Mitchell, who refused to accommodate any changes to their parenting plan, even when their son's extracurricular activities or medical appointments required adjustments.
- **Testing boundaries**—They may constantly test boundaries, making maintaining a stable co-parenting environment challenging. For example, Kelly's narcissistic ex, Tom, would frequently show up unannounced or attempt to take their children outside of the agreed-upon schedule, causing stress for Kelly and their children.
- **Breaking promises**—They may break promises and agreements when it suits them, causing confusion and instability for the children. For example, Laura's ex-husband, Jack, agreed to attend their daughter's dance recital but backed out at the last minute, disappointing their daughter and leaving Laura scrambling to rearrange her plans.
- **Making unilateral decisions**—They may make important decisions regarding the children without consulting you, undermining your role as a co-parent. For example, Sarah discovered that her ex, Paul, had enrolled their son in a new school without discussing it with her.

Emotional manipulation and mind games

- **Bad-mouthing**—They may bad-mouth you to the children or other people to undermine your relationship with them. For example, Karen found out that her ex-husband, Steve, would consistently speak ill of her to their children, blaming her for the divorce and portraying her as an unfit parent.

- **Manipulating**—They may manipulate the children to alienate you from them and create a rift in your relationship. For example, Jane often convinces her daughter, Lily, to lie to her father, Mike, about her whereabouts and activities. Jane does this to maintain Lily's loyalty and control their relationship, undermining Mike's trust in his daughter.
- **Exaggerating or withholding contributions**—They may exaggerate their financial contributions or withhold support to maintain control over the situation. For example, despite having a stable income, Jennifer's ex, Tim, would frequently delay or withhold child support payments, causing financial strain and tension for Jennifer.
- **Threatening**—They may make threats to force compliance from you, such as taking you to court or taking the children away. For example, George's ex, Rebecca, would withhold the children and threaten to fight for full custody if he didn't give her extra money on top of the court-agreed alimony.
- **Being overly sensitive**—They may be extremely sensitive to criticism but have no problem criticizing you in return. For example, whenever Zoe offered constructive feedback on their co-parenting arrangements, her ex, Josh, would become defensive and get unreasonably angry and upset.
- **Exploiting**—They may exploit their children's emotions for their own gain, using guilt or other tactics to

manipulate their children's feelings to achieve a desired outcome. For example, John tells his daughter Emily that if she doesn't want to spend time with him, it means she doesn't love him, making Emily feel guilty and forcing her to comply with his demands.

- **Gaslighting or confusing**—They may use gaslighting techniques to distort your or your children's reality, causing them to doubt their own experiences and memories. For example, Sarah would often criticize her son Michael but consistently denies ever saying hurtful things to him, insisting that he is imagining it or has a poor memory.
- **Projecting their issues**—They often project their own insecurities, fears, and failures onto their children, making them feel responsible for their parent's emotional state or well-being. For example, James, who struggles with his own ambition and work ethic, may call his daughter, Hannah, lazy and unmotivated, despite her being a well-performing child.

Involving the children

- **Being competitive**—They may try to compete with you for the children's affection, often through extravagant gifts or lax parenting. For example, Angela's ex, Peter, would consistently buy their children expensive gifts, allow them to stay up late, and skip chores, making Angela's consistent parenting seem strict and unreasonable.
- **Using children as messengers**—They may involve their children in adult matters by using them as go-betweens,

forcing them to relay information or communicate with the other parent on their behalf.

- **Ignoring or fighting arrangements**—They may ignore or fight agreed custody arrangements, creating instability and insecurity for the children. For example, despite agreeing on a shared custody schedule, Michelle's ex, Richard, would consistently try to renegotiate or disregard the agreed-upon terms, leading to constant conflict.
- **Prioritizing themselves**—They may often put their own wants or needs ahead of the children. For example, Frank's ex, Denise, would spend an hour getting herself ready before school and neglect helping the children with their uniform or lunch.
- **Being absent**—They may withdraw, disappear, or ignore the children completely, causing them emotional distress. For example, Mia's ex, Adam, would go for weeks without contacting their children, only to reappear and demand their attention on his terms.
- **Invading privacy**—They might invade your or your children's privacy by reading diaries, listening to phone calls, or snooping through personal belongings.

Co-parenting with a narcissist may resemble being in a boxing ring with someone who persistently hits below the belt, doesn't care about the rules, and just wants an easy win. If your child is subjected to these ongoing behaviors, it can result in low self-esteem, anxiety, emotional dysregulation, trust issues, self-doubt, depression, and destructive habits. Therefore, it is important to consider yourself both a skilled boxer who can duck, weave, and defend against attacks and a referee who is responsible for identifying when boundaries are crossed and the rules are broken. In this dual role, it's essential to know when to disengage and stop the fight, ensuring the well-being of everyone involved. You will learn more about boundary setting later in Chapter Six. But for now, let's first establish a strong foundation of resilience so you are in the best possible shape to deal with whatever is thrown at you—no matter what your co-parenting situation looks like.

BUILDING RESILIENCE

Building resilience is essential for thriving when co-parenting with a narcissist. By embracing the part of your dual role as a skilled boxer and a referee, you can grow stronger to better handle the ups and downs of raising children with your difficult ex-partner. Just as boxers train to withstand the punches and stress in the ring, you must also learn to protect yourself from the emotional blows that can arise in your co-parenting situation. Resilience is like robust fitness for a boxer because it's the foundation for all other skills. Without resilience, other techniques and strategies won't work as well. So let's first ensure you're in the best shape to face these challenges (Southwick & Charney, 2012).

Education

Learning as much as possible about your situation is important, as knowledge is power. The more you know about your ex's behavior, the better you'll understand their actions. And when you understand their actions, you'll be more equipped to handle the challenges that come your way. This book is a fantastic start, but you should not expect the learning to stop there. A list of further recommended resources is provided at the end of this book. There are also far more specific and nuanced topics regarding narcissists, which may apply to your situation. Everyone has unique circumstances, and after reading this book, you should consider something as specific as possible to those needs.

Restrict contact

You will stand a much better chance of remaining resilient if you stop draining your energy with unnecessary contact with your ex. Narcissists often have a strong desire for attention akin to that of toddlers—if they can't get the excessive admiration they want, they will respond in a way that may be emotionally distressing. They may attempt to provoke a reaction by prodding the boundaries because even negative attention is still attention in their eyes. By reacting to them, you give them the attention they crave, and they will keep returning for more. Try not to communicate with them unless it pertains directly to the children or is absolutely necessary. Avoid getting dragged into personal arguments or discussions about the past. Stick with written communication, such as email, texts, or a co-parenting app, wherever possible to keep things documented and objective. Avoid social media as it exposes you to your ex in many ways, such as through their posts, stories, and mutual friends. It gives them the information, ways, and means they could potentially use to generate conflicts or instigate unpleasant situations, sometimes publicly. Social media messaging apps also often can allow users to delete messages, and your ex may use this feature to their advantage. By unfriending or blocking your narcissistic ex, you can protect your privacy and mental well-being and avoid falling into the trap of social media confrontations.

Accept reality

Learn to accept what you cannot change. Narcissists tend to remain consistent in their behavior. Dealing with them may be highly frustrating because whatever you do and say, they will likely always see themselves as right. You can spend time crying in anger and frustration over this, but it won't help. In fact, dwelling on resentment will cloud your ability to deal with the situation with a level head. Even worse, bitterness can affect your children and their outlook on life too. Getting upset at a narcissist for exhibiting narcissistic behaviors is like getting upset at water being wet. It just is what it is, and there is no point assigning feeling or moral judgment to it. But with strong emotions and a long list of negative past experiences, it may be hard to reach acceptance.

If this is difficult, let yourself feel those negative emotions, describe them using words, and recognize their source. Are you feeling tense? Are you thinking, "It isn't fair"? If you are fighting against the situation, you are not accepting it. It also puts you in a worse-off state to deal with the situation. Take some deep breaths and try to let it go. See your ex's behavior as it is: out of your control. Remember that acceptance doesn't mean you are giving up; it just means you acknowledge that there are certain aspects you can't change.

Develop a broader perspective

When you look at things up close, they seem huge. And objects in the rearview mirror can appear closer than they are. If you constantly focus on every issue you've had with your ex, everything will feel worse than it is. Dwelling on past mistakes and decisions will hinder your ability to move forward.

Try to see the big picture in your life. Move your focus away from your troubles with your ex and onto something better, like enjoying the moment or planning something exciting for the future. Go out and have some fun. Chat with other people about their lives and their experiences. Or you could watch the news and realize that your situation may not be as bad as it seems when you think about it. Consider that you are one person in a big world, surrounded by countless others who face and overcome their own challenges. At the end of the day, your problems may not be as big as they seem or not unique to your situation.

Self-care

If you don't look after your house, what happens? Things start to fall apart. Windows leak, and the heating breaks down. Mold builds up in the shower. The garden becomes overgrown. Fixing those issues requires time and effort. Until then, everyone living there may get sick or injured. Similarly, if you don't take care of yourself, you risk illness, stress-related symptoms, and depression. This makes it much harder for you to bounce back after something negative happens, and your well-being directly impacts those around you, including your children.

So to maintain resilience—prioritize self-care. Truly, yourself, not the children. Self-compassion is a key component of well-being (Neff, 2011). Make sure to set aside time to do things that you enjoy. Maybe have a relaxing bath or play sports with your friends. You could listen to music or learn a language. Dedicate a few moments each day to do something just for you.

It goes without saying, but physical health is crucial. Exercise, a good diet, and sleep make it far easier to stay strong in difficult situations. Your ex may make you *want* to lie on the sofa eating ice cream, donuts, or chips, but it doesn't help you in the long run because a healthy body fosters a healthy mind. Regular exercise improves your physical strength and endurance and releases endorphins, which help reduce stress and boost your mood. Eating according to a balanced diet rich in nutrients ensures that your body and brain receive the fuel to function optimally—enhancing your ability to manage stress and maintain emotional stability—which you will need to deal with your ex-partner.

Positive mindset

The relationship between mental and physical health is deeply interconnected. When you take care of your body, you create a strong foundation for mental resilience. In turn, nurturing a positive mindset and practicing good self-care habits can motivate you to maintain a healthy lifestyle, forming an upward spiral. On the other hand, negative self-talk can harm your physical health as it increases stress levels. Chronic stress can weaken your immune system and cause headaches, muscle tension, and digestive problems. Additionally, it might lead to poor lifestyle choices like neglecting exercise and eating poorly, which can have detrimental long-term effects.

The good and bad news is that your brain isn't concerned with what is objectively true. Instead, it is more interested in the thought patterns you consistently focus on, and they influence you more. These recurring thoughts shape your perceptions of reality. A consistent practice of positive self-talk is essential to counteract negative thoughts and create an empowering mindset (Seligman, 2002), which is far more beneficial when facing challenges such as your difficult co-parenting situation.

So wouldn't you rather be thinking positive thoughts about yourself? Come up with some positive affirmations, and every time you find yourself thinking negatively, create positives that challenge and counteract them instead. For instance, if you often think, "I'm not good enough," replace it with, "I am worthy and capable."

This is not easy, as the brain will generally follow the path of least resistance. Think of it as a ski slope. Once you have been down the mountain a few times following the same route, tracks begin to form in the snow; and these tracks get deeper the more you use them. Though this makes it easy to get down the mountain, it becomes even harder to take another path. It is physically exhausting trying to turn your skis and take a different route. The brain works in much the same way. You become stuck on that path if you consistently think negatively and tell yourself you are no good. It becomes harder and harder for you to change direction and to think positively.

But the good news is that it can be done. You can form new tracks if you turn your skis and go down the other side of the mountain. If you make a conscious effort to think positively, eventually, your brain will go that way automatically. Each time you find yourself following a negative train of thought, change direction. Look for the positives in every situation (there's always something!). You could also try keeping a gratitude journal. There, write down a few things that you are grateful for or that have been positive each day. It may seem like a small exercise, but over time it will encourage your brain to look at life in a different way. Eventually, those tracks of positivity will become so well worn it will be difficult for you to think otherwise.

As you practice positive affirmations, visualize yourself successfully handling situations with your ex-partner. By mentally rehearsing positive outcomes, you can boost your confidence and reinforce your belief in your ability to cope with challenges.

Seek support

A problem shared is a problem halved. And believe me—there are many people out there who share your experiences and fully understand what you are going through. It can be hugely comforting and empowering to feel that you are not alone and have someone to turn to.

I know that it is sometimes easier said than done, but accept help when it is offered; you really don't have to do everything alone. Find someone who is understanding and willing to lend an ear when you need to express frustration. But remember, you don't always have to be talking about your issues. Just spending time with other people can help you to feel less isolated, even if you're sitting in silence. Take a moment to think of your social circles and who you can reach out to.

If you are struggling, do consider finding a therapist. Having someone neutral to listen to you can be a huge relief. A good therapist will help you work through some of your own issues and help you start to change your mindset to better cope with your situation. Support groups or online forums can also be valuable resources for sharing experiences and learning from others in similar situations. For this reason, while Chapter Four discusses therapy for your child, Chapter Five focuses on the importance of therapy for you to ensure you are a healthy parent to provide better support for your child.

A WORD ON REGRET

So, your ex is a narcissist. They act in a way that is unreasonable and self-centered and may refuse to discuss their behavior with you like a mature adult. You're also now a single parent who has to cope with the children and all their needs, the house, and your finances, and it's hard to find two minutes to yourself. It can be exhausting.

It would be easy to start wishing you had never had children in this situation, especially with your ex. This is not what parenthood is supposed to look like, and life would be much easier without them, right?

Well, let me share something with you. Every parent, everywhere, has felt this at some point. Even the ones without narcissistic exes. Everyone gets burnt out, exhausted, and overwhelmed with responsibilities and stress. Everyone has moments of selfishness just wanting five minutes of peace or a lie-in on the weekend or an all-inclusive trip to the Bahamas. Because everyone is human.

But it doesn't mean everyone doesn't love their children or that anyone would wish them away. Because they are all a gift, and despite all the stress and the hard work, they do bring a lot of joy.

It is normal to regret. You may regret your past decisions. You probably regret staying with your ex as long as you did. You probably regret having children with that person and not with someone else. But don't regret having the children themselves. Remember reading earlier about accepting reality? They are here now, so accept them and love them. Even if they may push your limits.

SUMMARY

Narcissism is a spectrum disorder, which means that individuals may exhibit varying degrees of narcissism, ranging from a few mild traits to severe narcissistic behaviors. Narcissists often believe that they are better and more important than everyone else. They may think and want to appear that they are never wrong, may need excessive admiration, and may lack empathy for others. They may be willing to take advantage of others to get what they want. These behaviors usually cover up deep-seated insecurities resulting from childhood trauma that narcissists work hard to hide.

Depending on your ex's level of narcissism, they may present some challenges regarding co-parenting. Because they may want to do things their way, they may disregard agreed-upon arrangements or make important decisions without consulting you. They are also likely to be resentful towards you for the breakup and may try to use the situation to retaliate; this could involve withholding finances, manipulating the children, or being inflexible and unsupportive.

Your first step in dealing with narcissistic behaviors is to build up your resilience. Reflect on the discussed areas and identify where you can improve. Implementing the following changes may help you build and maintain resilience:

- Prioritize self-care.
- Accept your reality and shift your perspective to a more positive outlook. (The more you work on these things, the easier it will be to deal with selfish actions and manipulation.)

- Get some support so that you are not facing the situation alone, and if you are struggling, consider therapy.
- Finally, remember to cherish your children. They are the silver lining in this challenging situation. Focus on the positives and love you share instead of the difficulties.

Now that you have a clearer understanding of narcissistic behaviors, the challenges they present in co-parenting, and a strong foundation of resilience, let's move on to Chapter Two, which focuses on specific techniques to use when dealing with your narcissistic ex-partner.

Action items

- Reach out to at least one friend or family member, share an experience related to your ex-partner, or seek advice on a problem you've been having with them. Even if the advice isn't perfect, the connection and support are invaluable.
- Write down the areas of resilience you identified as having room for improvement. Next to them, write the strategies you will implement to improve each one.

CHAPTER 2
YOUR RESPONSE TO THE NARCISSIST

DON'T FEAR THAT NARCISSIST

If your children are older than two, you will know what toddlers can be like. When my son was three, he was quite difficult. We were once in the supermarket doing our weekly shopping, and I told him that if he was good, he could have a small toy car as a reward. We got to the checkout, and he started running around, getting in everyone's way, and misbehaving. I told him to stop. He continued. I told him again, this time stating that if he didn't stop and behave, I would put the toy car back on the shelf. I continued to find his behavior bothersome, so I decided to put the toy car back. My son then had a tantrum, expressing his frustration through screaming, kicking, and flailing around until pretty much everyone in the supermarket looked at us with pity and annoyance. I'm sure you have been the parent in a similar situation or seen some other person struggling with a screaming child. Toddlers can be really hard work.

But what does this have to do with narcissists? Well, narcissists can be, in many ways, just like toddlers. They likely haven't developed the ability to understand that they are not the most important person in the world and that other people's feelings and needs are valid. Thus, they want to be able to behave as they please and to get what they want. And when someone challenges that, they often react strongly or become enraged. They probably no longer cry, scream, and flail on the floor. But if they think they aren't "winning," you will soon know about it.

And who's afraid of a big bad toddler? Nobody. Sure, they are hard work, and dealing with them can be emotionally and mentally draining. Sometimes you wish to just keep your head down and get your groceries without unnecessary drama. But are you scared of them? No. You set your boundaries and stick to them. When they get upset, you remain calm and stick to your guns. You positively phrase things and communicate with them in simple terms. You manage your expectations—you're not dealing with a mature adult; instead, you're dealing with someone whose behavior might resemble that of a three-year-old.

Embrace your inner strength when dealing with the narcissist in your life. While they may be exhausting to interact with, and you might unintentionally upset them, remember that it's not your responsibility to manage their emotions. Allow them to experience their feelings and stay focused on managing your expectations, establishing firm boundaries, and staying composed. You have the power to navigate these challenging interactions with resilience and poise.

HOW TO MANAGE A NARCISSIST

Unfortunately, since they are the parent of your child or children, you're more than likely stuck with them. When your child is old enough to be independent, you can throw a party because you will no longer have to deal with narcissistic dramas caused by the other parent. But for now, it is something you are going to have to deal with. So let's have a closer look at how to accomplish this.

Manage your expectations

It's very hard to reason well with a three-year-old. You can't *expect* them to do any different. You don't explain things to a three-year-old as you explain them to an adult because you don't *expect* them to understand. Bear that in mind when dealing with a narcissist. They may not operate as most mature, adult humans do, so don't *expect* them to. This realization will make your life a lot easier because it will remove some of the frustration and anger from your outlook.

Think about it this way. You order something online, and the confirmation email says you can expect your parcel in two days. Four days later, it hasn't turned up, and you're getting annoyed. Eight days later, you're angry and frustrated and probably on the phone trying to figure out where on earth it has got to. But if the confirmation email told you that the parcel would be delivered in eight days, you wouldn't spend the whole week getting annoyed that it wasn't here yet, because you weren't expecting it to be.

It is not that their behavior won't be challenging. You may occasionally want to bang your head against the wall. But try to set appropriate expectations. No matter how hard you try, they probably won't see things your way. They might not respond well to being directed or instructed. They likely won't admit when they are wrong. They often won't think about how you feel. So don't expect them to. It's not about letting them "get away" with their unacceptable behavior. It's about preparing yourself to deal with it.

Set boundaries

As a parent, you might worry about your child kicking off in the supermarket, and sometimes it is easier to placate them. They're starting to whine, so you give them a candy bar. Everyone has done it when they're tired and fed up and just want to sort the shopping out in peace. But as everyone also knows, if you give in to them every single time, you'll soon end up with a bigger problem.

Toddlers need boundaries. They need to know what you won't put up with under any circumstances. They may well test those boundaries, and they will probably get upset. But you must stick with them, or that toddler will soon have you wrapped around their little finger.

Again, narcissists might behave in a similar way. So set those boundaries. Tell them that you absolutely will not put up with distressing behavior and explain to them the consequences. If they are yelling at you down the phone, tell them you will not be shouted at and that you will hang up unless they are civil and respectful. If they carry on shouting, hang up the phone. Remember that if you keep letting them overstep those boundaries, it will only worsen in the long run. And yes, they may get upset. But their anger, frustration, or jealousy is their own emotion for them to deal with—it is not for you to manage. More on boundary setting will be discussed in Chapter Six.

Don't fight

Narcissists often crave attention, admiration, and a feeling that they are better than you. They thrive on emotional reactions. If they don't get these things (known as narcissistic supply), they will start to get restless or agitated.

Let's imagine that you are at home on Sunday with the children, maybe enjoying a pizza or a movie. Your ex is at home alone and has been all weekend. They might feel like they've had no one to tell them how amazing they are, no one to compare themselves to, and no one to give them any attention. Worse, they might be sitting there imagining how much fun you're all having and knowing how happy you are. So what do they do? How do they seek validation? They pick a fight. The next thing you know, they are on the phone telling you they can't have the children on Tuesday even though they know you're at work. Soon you're in the middle of a row, and before you know it, they have somehow managed to blame the whole situation on you. They say you are weak for being unable to take Tuesday off work, and if you were more assertive, it wouldn't be a problem. In their words, you are entirely unreasonable for not wanting to help them, and they make sure to let you know they aren't so petty and selfish. You come away from the conversation, saying you'll see what you can do and feeling miserable because they have once again managed to manipulate you. They end the conversation feeling satisfied because they've now had their need for attention and a sense of superiority.

It may sound all too familiar. What you must learn to do is not to fight. If your ex is in your face, making accusations or unreasonable demands, the worst thing you can do is to fight back. It will only ever end in an argument. They need you to fight back because then you are the one who lost control, and they can feel superior. So don't react, and don't fall into the trap of trying to explain to them why they are wrong. They can't be wrong, so they won't listen.

Instead, defuse the situation with minimal responses (see the section below on the grey rock method). Stick to your boundaries. These should have been drawn up in your parenting plan and signed by both of you. If they start trying to get an argument out of you by testing the boundaries, be firm but fair. In the example above, you might say, "We agreed in the parenting plan that Tuesdays were your responsibility. We also agreed that any changes would be agreed upon at least a week in advance. I'm afraid there is nothing I can do to help you this way."

Use the grey rock method

All children love candy. Adults probably all wish that children ate less of it, but obviously, if you keep giving it to them, they will keep asking you for it. When they develop a strong liking for it, they can be quite obnoxious if they don't get it. However, if you don't keep candy in the house, they are less likely to keep pestering you for it because they know it isn't readily available.

Narcissistic supply is much the same. If you consistently give a narcissist what they crave, they are only going to keep coming back and pestering you for more. If you cut off their supply, they should eventually get the message that the cupboard is bare and will look to get their supply elsewhere.

Cutting off their supply doesn't mean giving them silent treatment. Silent treatment involves completely ignoring someone or refusing to communicate, which is likely to anger your ex and escalate the situation. Instead, you could try using what is known as the grey rock method. Simply channel your best "grey rock" and be as boring and as uninteresting as possible. Use short, noncommittal answers which do not prompt any further debate. Rocks have no emotions, so don't show any. Likewise, speak in a neutral tone and don't show how you might feel inside. Don't give out any personal information. Minimize contact as much as you can—keep your texts very brief and don't linger on calls.

In theory, if you are consistently following the grey rock method, the narcissist may come to expect that they will get minimal responses and that they won't be able to get out of you what it is that they crave. It can be quite liberating, as it effectively gives you "permission" to step back from feeling that you need to make sure that you are saying the right thing and that you have to keep them happy. However, it can have some drawbacks. It is draining to maintain such a level of outward indifference, particularly in the face of extreme provocation. Left unchecked, this could take a toll on your mental health. It might also lead to an escalation on the narcissist's part, as they might become angered by it and increase their efforts to regain control. If your ex becomes excessively angry or abusive, you should be prepared to leave the situation and find somewhere safe. Prioritize your own safety and don't hesitate to call the police if necessary. While the grey rock technique is a powerful tool, it's also essential to be aware of the nonverbal signals you're sending. So let's take a closer look at body language.

Watch your body language

You might not have heard of Albert Mehrabian, but you might well have heard of his 7-38-55 theory of communication (Mehrabian & Wiener, 1967; Mehrabian, 1971). The theory states that there are three elements that help us understand what someone is communicating to us. They include:

- What is being said, which accounts for 7% of our understanding.
- How it is being said, which accounts for 38%.
- Body language, which accounts for 55%.

So, in face-to-face encounters, nonverbal cues are actually what you are paying the most attention to, whether you are aware of it or not. And so your body language really matters.

The challenge with body language is that, often, you are not aware of your actions. Your facial expressions, gestures, and movements can all occur subconsciously, so you may well appear aggressive, submissive, or disdainful to someone else without even realizing it.

Despite the difficulty, try to be aware of your body language when interacting with a narcissist. Again, think grey rock. Remain in a neutral posture. Try not to cower by lowering the chin, sloping the shoulders, or wrapping your arms around yourself. Equally, try not to appear aggressive. Don't raise your chin, puff out your chest, or fold your arms. Avoid gestures such as pointing or waving your arms around. Moreover, it can be difficult not to mirror the actions of someone who is angry and invading your space but try instead to maintain a neutral posture of calm confidence. Watch your facial expressions as well. Don't roll your eyes, sneer, or bare your teeth, for example. With an understanding of body language in mind, let's explore ways to cultivate calmness as a skill to better handle interactions with a narcissistic ex-partner.

DEVELOPING CALMNESS AS A SKILL

Remaining calm and neutral is hard work. You are programmed by years of evolution to respond to stressful situations with the fight-or-flight response. When faced with aggressive behavior, your body and mind naturally want to retaliate or withdraw. Make no mistake, it isn't easy to master your response to stress, so what can you practically do to develop calmness as a skill?

Behind the scenes

Meditation and mindfulness are powerful tools for reducing stress and managing emotions, particularly in the context of dealing with a narcissistic ex-partner. For instance, a 2019 paper analyses mindfulness meditation as an effective form of clinical intervention. Consistent application of mindfulness techniques can help alleviate stress and develop emotional regulation capacity, supporting the ability to remain calm (Wielgosz et al., 2019).

Meditation is often misunderstood as a practice to help you feel peace and tranquility right away. It may bring such results, but the real goal of meditation is to help you become more aware of your feelings and learn to accept them, whether good or bad. When you meditate, you practice paying attention to your thoughts and feelings without reacting or becoming overwhelmed. This helps you know yourself better and understand how you react to different situations. Over time, you may find that being more aware of your feelings helps you handle tough situations more easily. You may start to feel better, not because you're always happy, but because you can accept whatever feelings surface and know they won't last forever. So, meditation isn't just about feeling good right away. It's more like a way to help you get comfortable with your emotions and enjoy life in the present moment. And when you can do that, feeling good naturally follows.

Incorporating meditation into your daily routine doesn't require a significant time investment. Even just a few minutes each day or week can yield remarkable benefits. For those new to meditation, numerous apps or playlists are available to guide you through the process and help you develop a consistent practice. Alternatively, you can simply set aside a quiet space and time for yourself each day, focusing on your breath and allowing thoughts to come and go without judgment. In addition to meditation and mindfulness, practicing conversations can also help you feel more prepared and confident. Let's explore this idea further.

Learning your lines

Consider the preparation that actors undergo before performing on stage. There's the script, the decorations, the music, the costumes, the lighting, the staging, and the props. Actors put in a great deal of preparation to ensure they feel confident, calm, and composed when it's time to perform. Similarly, when dealing with a narcissistic ex-partner, you should invest time in preparing yourself mentally and emotionally. This will enable you to embody calmness and neutrality rather than merely pretending to be calm, even in the most challenging situations.

Actors need to rehearse, and similarly, you can benefit from practicing conversations with your ex. It may seem awkward, but stand in front of a mirror and envision various scenarios, determining what and how you will say it. Work on maintaining neutral responses and facial expressions. If you have a supportive friend or family member (not your children), you can practice these interactions with them. While you can't prepare for every situation, your ability to think critically is far stronger when you're not under stress, and this is a skill you can develop. Focus on staying calm and maintaining a low, steady voice during these practice sessions. In the thick of things, your practice will stand you in good stead.

Practice using "I" statements. For example, instead of saying, "You don't listen to me," try, "I feel not heard." This will help prevent you from sounding accusatory and enable you to state how you feel and what you need clearly. Avoid the use of absolutes such as always and never, which may only provoke a strong reaction. "You always talk over me" or "You never give me any money" will act as red rags to a bull. "I would appreciate it if you let me talk without interrupting" and "I need you to pay your share of the children's expenses" are clear and direct, without being confrontational. Having practiced your responses, you may still face anxiety when dealing with your narcissistic ex in real time. So let's discuss strategies for managing stress in the moment.

In the moment

You've done all the preparation, and you've practiced your part thoroughly. But you may still feel the rush of adrenaline if your ex starts to provoke you. So what can you do to remain calm when the curtain goes up?

Take some deep breaths. Breathing deeply and slowly tells the body to stop releasing stress hormones and calm down. It also gives you a chance to gather your thoughts and think more clearly about how you are going to respond.

While you are breathing deeply, consciously relax your body. When you're anxious, you tend to tense your muscles, which can exacerbate feelings of stress. Take a moment to focus on each area of your body, attempting to release the tension.

Redirect your negative energy towards something neutral, such as a piece of furniture or a point on the wall. When you feel overwhelmed and in danger of losing your composure, mentally direct all your negativity to that spot. Although it may sound unconventional, this technique can be effective in helping you maintain your calm.

THE IMPORTANCE OF PROPER DOCUMENTATION

Narcissists are often excellent at manipulation. They may have a knack for twisting discussions or situations to serve their own interests and may be highly skilled at gaslighting, making you doubt yourself. You may have experienced this before: you enter a conversation with a clear understanding of the truth and a plan to convince them, but within minutes, they've managed to persuade you that you're wrong and they're right. Even worse, they may make you feel guilty for doubting them and leave you feeling small and inadequate compared to their perceived wisdom and knowledge. That's why it's so important to document everything. Without documentation, they can easily manipulate situations to their advantage. If something is written down, it is much harder for them to dispute it.

Chapter Seven will cover the importance of having a written parenting plan agreed upon and signed by both parties. However, consider taking this a step further by keeping most of your ongoing communication in writing. Emails or text messages can both be saved and referred to at a later date. If your ex calls with a request or mentions something, perhaps when you are busy picking up the children and likely distracted, don't engage. Ask them to send the request via message instead.

If you do need to meet face-to-face with your ex, it is advisable to take a neutral party with you to avoid a he-said-she-said situation. You could record conversations on your phone or another device for later reference. If they do not agree to you doing this, inform them you will be making notes during the meeting for them to review and sign afterwards.

It might also be helpful to keep notes on your interactions, including requests, kept and missed appointments, comments they make, and so on. Ensure these are filed well or make a note of where you have saved them for easy access in the future.

Treating co-parenting as a business partnership

Although it may seem excessive, treat your co-parenting relationship like a business partnership. Businesses document everything to keep their projects moving forward. Documenting protects them legally and provides employees with a behavioral framework. Approach your co-parenting as if you were the secretary for an important company tasked with taking notes and filing everything discussed by the board. This approach will help streamline your co-parenting arrangements, provide protection in case of disputes, and may potentially encourage your ex to maintain appropriate behavior.

SUMMARY

Dealing with narcissists can be challenging. While you may see yourself as a parent who just wants to keep their head down and get your groceries, their behavior might resemble a toddler having a tantrum in a supermarket because they are not getting their own way or enough attention. When they're causing trouble, it's crucial for you to act firmly but calmly, like a composed parent. Avoid pandering to their demands and establish clear boundaries with consequences for poor behavior. Don't fight or argue with them, as this only adds fuel to their fire. Instead, be a neutral grey rock—give minimal responses and show no emotion.

Maintaining composure and neutrality when interacting with your ex reduces the likelihood of them seeking their narcissistic supply from you. While working on improving your response to your narcissistic ex-partner, it's crucial to understand the potential impact of their behavior on your child. Next chapter, "The Impact of Being Raised by a Narcissist on Your Child," will explore in-depth the challenges and long-term effects that children may face when growing up with a narcissistic parent, along with strategies for supporting them through this difficult experience.

Action items

- Work on your body language and overall composure. Use a confident stance, hold brief eye contact, and maintain a neutral facial expression. Additionally, focus on remaining calm and collected during interactions with your ex. Practice this in front of a mirror or with a trusted friend until it becomes second nature. This will reduce the likelihood of your ex using you for narcissistic supply.
- Practice the grey rock method in your conversations with your ex. Keep your responses brief and factual,

avoiding personal details or emotional reactions. The more you do this, the better you'll become at managing your own internal expectations during these interactions. This approach will also encourage a more positive mindset when dealing with your ex.

- Include mindfulness, steady breathing, meditation, and internal relaxation techniques in your daily routine. This can help you manage stress and maintain focus. There are numerous apps and resources that can guide you in this. With consistent practice, these techniques may help you maintain composure in the presence of your ex.
- Ensure you thoroughly document all interactions with your ex-partner. Where possible, stick to written communication to create a clear record. Also, be sure to review your current methods of communication to see if any changes need to be made. Write down the details of every encounter, noting the date, time, and what transpired. Store these notes in a secure location and consider making backup copies. If you haven't already, prepare a note-taking system before proceeding to the next chapter.

CHAPTER 3
THE IMPACT OF BEING RAISED BY A NARCISSIST ON YOUR CHILD

IS NARCISSISM A GENETIC DISORDER

Figuring out how much genetics play a part in personality traits like narcissism can be very hard. It's easier to understand how genes with physical manifestations, like those determining eye color or chances of getting certain diseases, are hereditary. But when it comes to personality, many other factors come into play.

Research does suggest that narcissistic traits are moderately heritable (Luo et al., 2014; Kendler et al., 2008). However, it's important to remember that narcissism is a complex personality type with many different aspects. Even if someone has a genetic risk for narcissistic traits, their upbringing and life experiences will play a bigger part in shaping their personality. This means a person could end up with NPD, just a few narcissistic traits, or none at all.

For instance, a 2018 study published in the *Journal of Affective Disorders* revealed that genetic factors account for approximately

24% of the variation in traits related to NPD. This finding supports the idea that genetics contribute to the development of narcissism, but they are not the only determining factor. Environmental influences, such as upbringing, relationships, and life experiences, also play a significant role.

The following sections concentrate on those environmental factors on which you can make the most impact—your child's upbringing and their relationships, particularly the relationships they have with their parents. They will explore how these factors affect your child and discuss strategies to mitigate the negative consequences.

SO, WILL YOUR CHILD BECOME A NARCISSIST TOO

If genetics doesn't have a huge hand in the development of narcissism, what does? Studies have shown that there are three main reasons why children may develop narcissistic behaviors—and all directly relate to their parents' behavior:

1. Their parents treat them as better and more deserving than others. The children then grow up with an overinflated sense of self, believing they are better and more entitled than others. In a study conducted on 565 children aged 7–12, it was concluded that the more parents believed their child to be special, the more they developed narcissistic tendencies (Brummelman et al., 2015).
2. Their parents only give love conditionally, based on their achievements. They are praised when they achieve and punished when they do not. This may lead them to

continually strive for excellence, and anything less will not do. They have higher chances of becoming overachieving perfectionists who cannot tolerate their flaws and consequently can't cope with anyone else's either.

3. Their parents devalue their achievements, continually put them down, or ignore them completely. Nothing the child does is ever considered good enough, and thus, they may grow up feeling devalued and unloved. This sometimes leads to them becoming overachievers to "prove their parents wrong." They may continue to strive to win the love and admiration of their narcissistic parent long after they are grown up and to continually show the world that they are the best. Children of narcissistic parents often grow up to be quite angry and spiteful, and anyone who reminds them of their parent, perhaps by pointing out a shortcoming, may also become a target of their resentment.

At the end of the day, it boils down to children recreating what they see their parents doing. Growing up with someone who doesn't demonstrate a consistent, caring attitude, empathy towards others, and self-acceptance (flaws and all) is more likely to grow up with the same behaviors. They mimic observed actions of the adults in their life, or to put it more plainly—monkey see, monkey do.

However, it's not a foregone conclusion that narcissists produce narcissists. Studies have shown that while the children of narcissists may develop other issues and disorders, less than half become narcissists (Durvasula, 2017). Furthermore, if the child develops just one secure attachment with a parent, the risk of their developing NPD or a number of other disorders is *greatly* diminished.

You have taken the first important step in removing yourself from your narcissistic ex because you recognize the need to protect yourself and your children. With that conviction, you have the strength and the means to provide your children with what they need to counteract the narcissistic influence. More on this in Chapter Five.

HOW ELSE CAN NARCISSISTIC ABUSE AFFECT YOUR CHILD EMOTIONALLY

As children grow and develop, they rely on their parents as role models to learn how to function in the world. This includes learning essential skills such as communication, cooperation, empathy, influence, trust, and developing self-belief and self-love. When a child's primary role model is a narcissistic parent, they may inadvertently learn the wrong lessons. If a parent only shows love when the child pleases them, the child learns to conditionally love others as well. Similarly, if the parent lacks empathy towards others, the child is likely to adopt this lack of empathy in their interactions with people.

Unfortunately, there's no way to sugarcoat the fact that narcissistic behavior can cause a range of emotional and behavioral problems for children, both in the short and long term (Livesley et al., 2018). So let's have a closer look at these potentially damaging effects.

Low self-esteem

Children who have been brought up to believe that their desires, needs, and actions don't matter are likely to grow up with the same belief, developing harsh inner critics that tell them they're not good enough.

Anxiety and emotional dysregulation

Children that are continually on edge because of constant emotional turmoil may end up experiencing chronic anxiety. They often feel the need to be on high alert, anticipating the unpredictable moods and demands of their narcissistic parent. This heightened state of anxiety can manifest in various ways, such as generalized anxiety, social anxiety, or panic attacks. Over time, this constant state of worry can become deeply ingrained, leading to difficulty relaxing, problems with sleep, and even physical symptoms like headaches or digestive issues.

Trust issues

The unpredictable and manipulative behavior of a narcissistic parent can make it difficult for a child to feel secure in their relationships with others. They may become overly cautious, fearing that others will betray or hurt them in the same way their narcissistic parent did. Trust issues can negatively impact a person's ability to form healthy, lasting relationships and can contribute to feelings of isolation and loneliness.

Self-doubt

Narcissists can teach children not to trust their own inner voices and doubt everything they believe. As a result, they grow up constantly second-guessing themselves, which means they may struggle to make decisions or take appropriate risks later in life.

Self-sabotage

Self-sabotage involves thoughts or actions that undermine one's success or well-being, sometimes occurring subconsciously.

They stem from deep-rooted beliefs or insecurities. This can manifest as procrastination, perfectionism, self-destructive habits, and a fear of failure or success. In extreme cases, the individual will continuously go through cycles of "success," then self-sabotage as their validation comes from "earning it" again.

People-pleasing

Children who have grown up forced to worship their parents and neglect their own needs may grow up to become people pleasers. Where they have grown up with a parent with unpredictable moods and angry outbreaks, they may do anything to avoid conflict in future relationships, even at their own expense.

Depression and numbness

The continual barrage of different emotions expressed by a narcissistic parent may lead to their children's depression or emotional numbness. This coping mechanism may develop to protect themselves from further emotional pain. Narcissists often cause their children to become self-isolated or invalidate their feelings, exacerbating these issues. This can cause persistent sadness, hopelessness, and a lack of interest in activities once enjoyed or a disconnection from emotions, making it difficult to feel love or joy.

Destructive habits

Destructive habits can emerge in children of narcissistic parents to cope with the emotional distress they experience. These habits may include substance abuse, compulsive behaviors, self-harm, or engaging in toxic relationships. Often, these behaviors help temporarily escape emotional pain but perpetuate a cycle of harm and emotional distress.

HOW NARCISSISTIC ABUSE CAN AFFECT YOUR CHILD'S FUTURE RELATIONSHIPS

The problems mentioned above can significantly impact a person's future relationships in various aspects of life, including friendships, work associations, romantic relationships, and family connections. They often stem from the attachment style one learns as a child.

Attachment styles

From the moment you are born, you depend on your parents to provide your basic needs, such as shelter, warmth, and food. You also rely on them as a source of comfort when you are upset or distressed. Your parents' responsiveness and ability to meet your needs shape your attachment style. Although it is possible to change attachment style (with a lot of hard work and self-reflection), the one you develop as a child will usually persist into adulthood and dictate your relationships with others. There are four main attachment styles: secure, anxious/preoccupied, dismissive-avoidant, and fearful-avoidant/disorganized (Ainsworth et al., 1978).

Secure attachment

Those with a secure attachment style have good self-esteem. They are independent and not reliant on others but are equally happy to open up and share their emotions. They love and accept love readily and value relationships and social support.

Anxious/preoccupied attachment

This attachment style generally arises when parents are somewhat unpredictable—sometimes meeting the child's needs and sometimes ignoring them. Those with an anxious or preoccupied attachment style typically have low self-esteem. They constantly worry that their partners don't love them and can often be clingy and desperate. They fear being alone and require constant validation and support, needing others to show them proof of their love and commitment. They tend to be very distraught when relationships end.

Dismissive-avoidant attachment

When the parents do not meet a child's needs, the child learns to be self-reliant and grows up to be distrustful of others. Those with the dismissive-avoidant attachment style generally have high self-esteem and don't feel they need much social support. They are very independent and unwilling to open up to others. They shy away from relationships as they do not want to be dependent on or overly attached to anyone else.

Fearful-avoidant/disorganized attachment

This attachment style can arise when a child has very unpredictable parents. Sometimes, they act very lovingly, and sometimes, they are erratic—perhaps behaving strangely or becoming angry. The child is both comforted by and fearful of the parent. In this scenario, they will likely grow up to crave attention and love and be fearful of intimacy. They may want social connection but prefer to be alone and can be easily emotionally overwhelmed. They generally will avoid relationships and depend on others through fear that they will be let down.

Narcissistic parents tend to be unpredictable—often disregarding their children's needs one moment and adoring them the next. If the child pleases them, they are praised lavishly; if they don't, they are shouted at or punished. When children are both fearful of and comforted by their parents, it's no surprise that they almost always develop fearful-avoidant attachment styles. They may crave love, affection, and close friendships but simultaneously may be afraid to open up to others for fear of being hurt.

Childhood trauma

It is often believed that people grow up to marry someone like their mother or father, subconsciously seeking out those with traits like their parents. When encountering these traits in someone new, they may feel connected and safe because they appear familiar.

This can be positive if someone grew up with loving and empathetic parents and later seeks out partners with the positive traits their parents displayed. But what if they grew up with a narcissistic parent? They may either recognize the abusive traits and avoid potential partners displaying them or, unfortunately, be drawn to those individuals because they feel familiar and safe, thus replicating their childhood environment.

A challenging mix

Having a narcissistic parent may result in developing a fearful-avoidant attachment style, trust issues, low self-esteem, indecisiveness, persistent self-doubt, and difficulties processing emotions. It's easy to see how these factors can negatively affect someone's relationships. Even if they manage to avoid falling for someone who behaves just like their narcissistic parent, they are likely to struggle to form and maintain healthy, meaningful relationships.

MITIGATING THE EFFECTS OF HAVING A NARCISSISTIC PARENT

At this point, you may be feeling disheartened, fearing that your child's chances of a happy, fulfilling social and romantic future have been irreparably harmed. But don't worry. Research indicates that just one secure attachment in a child's life can effectively shield them against the negative effects of narcissism: "Close, warm, affectionate and secure attachment leads to children who have the capacity to love others" (Durvasula, 2017).

You may feel like you are sending your child out into the cold every time they go to their other home, worrying their hearts will eventually freeze over and become hardened to love or self-belief. But every time they return to you, your positive influence can serve as a buffer, offering the emotional equivalent of a warm hug, hot chocolate, and a cozy blanket. Just like a daily dose of vitamins, your mature, stable, level-headed presence can help ward off the negative effects of narcissism.

It's important to acknowledge that narcissism, like many personality traits, exists on a spectrum. While the behavior of a narcissistic parent can have damaging effects, they may still be capable of forming positive relationships with their children. This doesn't mean their actions are without consequence, but it does complicate the situation and provide some hope.

And remember, it's not just you. There are very likely other supportive, emotionally sensitive people in your child's life. Consider their grandparents, aunts, uncles, family friends, and teachers. Your child is likely surrounded by multiple people who provide a strong positive impact on their emotional well-being.

Practical steps to help your child

1. **Build your own resilience first**—Remember Chapter One? Ensuring you are emotionally strong will set a good example for your child and allow you to provide the support they need.
2. **Model good behaviors**—Show your child what a supportive, empathetic, and loving parent looks like.
3. **Surround your children with good people**—Encourage relationships with positive role models, such as relatives, family friends, or teachers who can provide guidance and emotional support.
4. **Sign them up for confidence-boosting activities**—Participate with your child or enroll them in activities encouraging socialization, building healthy relationships, and developing positive skills. Consider scouting, sports, drama, dance, or music—whatever aligns with their interests.
5. **Encourage their opinions**—Ask for their input in the daily running of the house and engage in conversations about various topics, such as world events, TV shows, or school life. This will help them open up, think critically and decisively, and express their feelings.
6. **And most importantly, teach your child empathy**—Help them understand the importance of being kind, compassionate, and considerate towards others. This crucial skill will positively impact their relationships and emotional well-being.

DEVELOPING EMPATHY IN YOUR CHILD

Empathy is the ability to understand and share someone else's feelings, essentially putting yourself in their shoes. It involves relating your own experiences and emotions to those of others, allowing you to connect with them on a deeper level.

Empathy is important as it influences your behavior towards others. Understanding the emotions related to being insulted or let down makes us less likely to impose such feelings on others. On the contrary, experiencing kindness and respect may encourage us to treat others similarly.

Empathy and the narcissist

Narcissists often struggle with empathy. Those with NPD may not be able to appreciate others' emotions because they tend to solely focus on themselves. As a result, they may hurt or betray others to get what they want, as they may not care about the impact their actions have on other people.

People with less severe narcissism might have some understanding of others' feelings, but they often find a way to make the situation about themselves. For example, you come home from a particularly bad day at work. You offload to your partner, and they say, "Well, at least it's the weekend now," and continue doing what they were doing. Or maybe they say, "Yeah, I know how you feel—my boss is always doing xyz…," and proceed to talk about their work for the next 20 minutes. Or, maybe they start looking at recruitment websites, telling you that you need a new job.

In all of these examples, dismissing your experience, shifting the conversation to themselves, or trying to impose a solution, the narcissist has shown they struggle to genuinely empathize with your emotions. Rather than considering the feelings and perspectives of others, their focus is typically on how situations affect them personally. This self-centered approach can introduce significant challenges in forming healthy relationships or receiving genuine support from narcissists, highlighting the importance of fostering and nurturing empathy throughout your child's development.

Why should you teach your child empathy

There are multiple reasons why encouraging empathy in your child is essential:

- **Reducing narcissistic tendencies**—By nurturing empathy in your child, you can help prevent the development of narcissistic traits. As your child learns to appreciate the emotions of others, they are less likely to focus solely on themselves.
- **Forming meaningful relationships**—Empathy plays a vital role in forming and maintaining healthy relationships while prioritizing the well-being of others. When your child can understand and empathize with others, they are more likely to develop strong, balanced connections with friends, family members, and romantic partners throughout their lives.
- **Developing emotional intelligence**—Teaching your child empathy will help them better understand and navigate the emotions of those around them. They will be able to respond appropriately to others' feelings, leading to more effective communication and conflict resolution.

- **Recognizing inappropriate behaviors**—Developing empathy will support your child's potential to identify unhealthy or toxic behaviors in others, including those of a narcissistic parent. This awareness will help them set boundaries and seek support when necessary, protecting their own emotional well-being.
- **Showing compassion and kindness**—As children become capable of understanding and empathizing with the emotions of others, they will learn the positive and emotional impacts of kindness and compassion. By teaching your child empathy, you are helping to create a more caring and supportive world.

How to teach your child empathy

There are strategies you can implement to foster empathy in your child. I've listed some of them below—they encourage your child to consider the feelings and perspectives of others and how their actions may affect them.

- **Model empathy**—Show your child what empathy looks like in action. Let them see you helping others or talking to grandma about her problems. Let them see you crying at that sad movie on TV. Any time you show that you understand how others are feeling may encourage them to do the same.
- **Discuss feelings**—Encourage them to see that you are a person, too, not just Mom or Dad. Tell them when their behavior makes you feel angry or sad. Also, tell them when their behavior makes you happy.
- **Develop understanding**—If they mistreat another child, don't just force them to say sorry—children will often

repeat the words without understanding what they mean. Instead, ask them to consider how their actions have made that child feel.

- **Validate emotions**—Try not to punish or dismiss anger or sadness. Let them feel what they are feeling and tell them you understand. You can address the underlying issues when they are feeling calmer.
- **Read stories**—Expose your child to stories that explore feelings and relationships. There are so many brilliant children's books for all ages. This will help children think about how other people feel and expose them to various people or situations they do not usually encounter.
- **Role-play emotions**—For younger children, you could play a game of guessing the emotion—you act out a feeling and have them guess how you are feeling. Get them to do the actions as well. For slightly older children, you could try playing with different scenarios or adding emotions to the pretend play. For teenagers, you could encourage them to join drama groups.
- **Praise caring actions**—Acknowledge or praise your child when they have been caring or have thought about others. Praising children for their great drawing or for winning a football match is easy. But don't forget to praise them for looking after their siblings or friends, for instance, "You were really kind when Jodie fell over today. I'm sure she felt better when you gave her a hug."
- **Encourage relationships**—Ask lots of questions about their friends and classmates. Getting them to think about what their friends think and feel about things will help ensure that they are focusing on other people and themselves.

- **Promote helpfulness**—Let them know how their help supports you. Get your child involved in helping at home and in the community, emphasizing their actions' positive impact on others.

Challenges teaching empathy amidst narcissistic influence

Teaching empathy to children can present unique challenges, especially when a narcissistic parent's influence is strong. Narcissistic parents may undermine or contradict the empathetic values you are trying to instill in your child, leading to confusion and mixed messages. In such cases, it's essential to remain patient and consistent in your efforts to promote empathy in your child. You may need to have ongoing conversations with your child, addressing any conflicting information or behaviors they witness and helping them understand why empathy is important. Additionally, it's crucial to maintain open communication and create a safe environment where your child feels comfortable discussing their feelings and experiences. In some instances, you might need to involve a professional therapist or counselor to provide additional support and guidance for you and your child. Therapists are discussed in greater detail in the next chapter.

SUMMARY

Children with a narcissistic parent can face numerous emotional challenges, including low self-esteem, anxiety, depression, trust issues, people-pleasing tendencies, and destructive behaviors. They are more likely to develop a fearful-avoidant attachment style, which involves simultaneously craving social connection and cutting themselves off for fear of being hurt. Additionally, they are at risk of becoming narcissistic themselves through learned behavior or to compensate for the absence of unconditional love.

However, just one stable, secure attachment can greatly mitigate the negative effects of narcissism. As a parent, you can play a significant role in enabling your child to develop the ability to form healthy and secure relationships.

As you continue to support your child in dealing with the potential challenges posed by a narcissistic parent, it's essential to take proactive measures to ensure their safety and well-being. Chapter Four will explore strategies for protecting your children from the harmful effects of narcissistic behavior and fostering their emotional resilience.

Action items

- Observe the narcissistic parent's interactions with your child and make a note of any patterns or specific behaviors that are harmful or manipulative. These behaviors may constitute focal points you can support your child with, compensating for areas where the narcissistic parent may fall short.
- Encourage open communication with your child by actively listening, validating their feelings and experiences, and offering support. This will promote an environment where your child feels comfortable expressing their thoughts and emotions.
- Celebrate your child's achievements and encourage their efforts. Providing positive reinforcement where appropriate will foster their self-esteem and counter

negativity they may have received from the narcissistic parent.

- Write down the strategies you will implement to teach your child empathy. Include methods you will use to record their implementation and your child's response and progress over time.

CHAPTER 4
PROTECTING YOUR CHILDREN FROM THE EFFECTS OF SEPARATION AND ABUSE

DIVORCE IS HARD ENOUGH FOR A CHILD

The separation of any family can be an emotionally challenging and life-changing event for children, and many factors contribute to its impact on their well-being. Children often struggle to understand the reasons behind their parents' separation and may mistakenly believe it is their fault. The repercussions of divorce can manifest in various ways, including behavioral issues, poor academic performance, mental health challenges, and relationship difficulties in adulthood.

Research indicates that, under certain circumstances, the negative effects of divorce on children's educational attainment can be greater than if a parent passes away. Even though both events cause challenges and stressors in a child's life, divorce often also combines conflict, abandonment, and feelings of rejection that can leave lasting emotional scars (Amato, 2001).

The reasons behind this decline include a possibly reduced standard of living, impaired parenting due to stressed parents, decreased parental supervision and time spent with children, and being caught in the middle of a conflict between the parents in the postdivorce years (Amato & Sobolewski, 2001). Additionally, children may face disruptions, such as relocating to new neighborhoods and schools or adjusting to their parents' new partners.

In comparison to other disruptive life events, divorce often involves a higher level of interpersonal conflict and emotional turmoil. Parental incarceration, military deployment, or migration can create feelings of loss and separation, but they often lack the resulting intense feelings of rejection and abandonment that children may experience during a divorce.

Therefore, it's easy to see why so many people out there believe that parents should stay together "for the sake of the children," but this is not always the best solution, as conflict and emotional turmoil are the root causes of these problems. In fact, two stable, peaceful homes are far better for a child's well-being than one filled with constant conflict (Amato & Sobolewski, 2001). It is crucial for parents to prioritize their children's needs during this transition and make informed decisions to minimize potential harm.

In my counseling experience, children's difficulties arise from how parents handle various aspects of divorce rather than the divorce itself. And how you, as a parent undergoing separation from your narcissistic partner, manage them is what matters, which is well within your control. By understanding the unique impact of divorce and addressing the specific stressors it introduces, you can better support your children's emotional well-being during this difficult time.

HELP YOUR CHILD UNDERSTAND THE SITUATION

Make no mistake—separation is going to be hard on you all. Chapter One made some suggestions about how you can boost your own resilience in this challenging time, but what can you do to help your children? Unfortunately, you cannot control your ex's behavior or how they handle the situation with your children. However, you can manage your own behavior, and you can be the force that your children need during this difficult time.

1. **Be reliable.** Children need assurance that their parents are there for them and that their love will remain, even if their parents no longer love each other. In the face of an unreliable ex-partner who may be absent for weeks, months, or even years, it is crucial for you to be consistent and dependable. Keep your promises. Maintain open communication. Show up.
2. **Don't freeze your ex out.** It may be tempting to remove all contact with your ex and stop them from seeing your children. After all, you are all too familiar with their narcissistic ways. If they are not being abusive (discussed later in the chapter), and they are making an effort and asking to see their children, let them.
3. **Be open and honest.** Tell the truth about what happened and answer children's questions honestly. However, do remember that their age will have an impact on what they can understand. For little ones, keep it simple and

don't bombard them with too much information. For older children, you can explain a bit more, but be sure you are not overburdening them or using them to offload your problems— to vent your emotions choose someone from your list in Chapter One instead.

4. **Reassure and repeat.** Children often feel as though the breakup is because of something they did or didn't do. Tell them you love them and reassure them, both with words and physical affection. Repeat the things they need to hear and answer the same questions again and again. But don't give them false hopes—make sure they know that the separation is final.
5. **Stay calm and be patient.** Remember that you can't change their emotions. They may be angry or sad for a while. Younger children may cry and be overly dependent. There may struggle to express their emotions in a calm way or to maintain their sleep patterns. Older children may become withdrawn or may "act out." Just take some deep breaths and try not to get upset or angry with them. Be understanding and patient. It will soon pass.
6. **Stick to the routine.** Where possible, keep routines and rituals the same. If they always have a story before bedtime, don't change it. If they always come into your bed in the morning for a cuddle, stick with it. Children need these little routines as anchors to feel secure and reassured that even though big things are changing, other things will stay the same.
7. **Don't fight.** You may struggle to get along with your ex, but as much as possible, don't argue in front of the children. Talk kindly about the other parent or say nothing. Of course, you can't control your ex's behavior,

but you can avoid reacting to them or engaging in arguments while the children are there.

8. **Promote adaptability.** During times of change, help your child understand that change is a natural part of life and that adapting to new situations is an essential skill. Encourage them to be open-minded and flexible and to embrace new experiences with curiosity and positivity. Provide them with various opportunities to try new activities, meet new people, and learn from different environments. Reinforce their adaptability by praising their willingness to adapt and emphasizing the importance of being open to change.

COMMON QUESTIONS AND SUGGESTED RESPONSES

Based on numerous consultations with divorced parents, the following questions have been identified as those most frequently asked by children during a divorce. Here are some recommended ways to address these concerns:

Why are you getting divorced/moving out/splitting up?

- Mommy and Daddy can't live in the same house without arguing anymore. We will all be happier if we live in different houses. Remember, we will always be your Mom and Dad wherever we live, and we still love you.
- We've tried, but we just can't get along anymore, and it's taking a toll on everyone. It will be better for us and you if we are apart. But we still love you, and it will all be ok.

Was it something I did?/Is it my fault?

- Absolutely not. You are wonderful, and we love you very much.
- These are adult problems, and none of it is your fault. We are very proud of you.

Why don't you love Daddy/Mommy anymore?

- I will always love Daddy / Mommy because he / she helped me make you. But sometimes, even when grown-ups love each other, they can't stay married. We will both always love you because that kind of love is forever.
- You don't just stop loving someone, but I don't love them the way I used to. Adult relationships are complicated, but the love I have for you is pure and will never change.

Will you get back together?

- No. I know that's sad, but we will all be happier this way.
- No, I know it's hard for you, and you really want your family all together, but that isn't going to happen. I will be there to help you, and when you get used to it, you'll be happy again.

Will I still go to the same school/preschool?

- You may need to switch to a different school. I know that might be scary, but you will get to make lots of new friends, and I will help you.
- You might need to move to a new school, and it's normal to feel anxious. You're awesome, and you'll soon make new friends.

Will we have to move house?

- We will need to find a new house! Let's draw a picture of what we would like it to look like.
- Yes, we will be moving house. I'll need your help in looking at places so that we can find somewhere that we all really love.

Why can I eat on the sofa/stay up till 10 pm when I'm at Mom's but not at yours?

- Mom makes the rules in her house, but I have my own rules here. We'll make a list and stick them on the fridge so you can remember them.
- What goes on at Mom's house is up to her, but these are the rules we all agree to stick to here.

When am I going back to Dad's/Mom's?

- You've got three sleeps here, and then you'll be back at Mom's. What fun things shall we do while you are here?
- You're back there on Friday. We'll mark all the days on the calendar, so you can see exactly what you're doing.

Of course, there will be other questions. Children sometimes worry about things you may overlook or just don't consider important. Just remember:

- **Repetition may be necessary**—Some parents have noticed that their children continue to ask questions or seek reassurance, even years after the divorce.
- **Be honest**—You don't have to tell them absolutely everything, but make sure what you do tell them is true.
- **Consider your audience**—What you say (and how you say it) to a four-year-old will be very different from what you say to a fourteen-year-old.
- **Don't take it personally**—One Dad told me that his five-year-old would ask when he was going back to his Mom's the minute he arrived from her house. At first, he felt sad and that his son would rather be there than with him, but later he realized that his son just felt confused and wanted information about what was happening and when.
- **Be proactive**—You can stave off some questions by providing information in advance. For example, mark when they will be going to their other home on a calendar so they can count the days.
- **Reassure**—Make sure you end your responses with reassurance.

FURTHER IDEAS FOR HELPING YOUR CHILDREN ADJUST

For children aged six years and under:

1. Build two blanket forts. Call one of them Mom's house and the other Daddy's house. Play at going between the two, doing normal things like having a (pretend) tea, and then going to bed.
2. Draw pictures of their two homes.
3. Make a big timetable or calendar with all the days of the week. Stick pictures of Mom/Dad on the days they will be at each house.

For children aged 7 to 13:

1. Make a wish list of everything they would like for their new house. You could cut pictures out of magazines or get them to write it down. It doesn't have to be entirely realistic!
2. Sit down together and agree on some rules for your house. Make them positive rather than negative statements, for example, you could decide: "We will look after each other" (rather than "No hitting"), or "We will tell the truth" (rather than "No lying").

Have everyone (including you) agree by signing it. The rules may be different at their other home, but it will help them be clear about what you expect.

1. Give your children a worry worm or a worry jar. Encourage them to tell their worries to the worm before bedtime or to write things down and put them in the jar. They might want to do it by themselves, which will help them not to bottle things up. Or if you are there, you can talk to them about their concerns.

For teens:

1. Give them some small chores to do around the house. This will help them to feel involved in their new home and something to focus on. Be sure to give plenty of praise when they do a good job.
2. Encourage them to keep a journal as a release for their emotions. But don't be tempted to read it!
3. Help them with the practicalities of moving between houses. They might be worried about having everything they need for school on the right day. You could try keeping all their schoolbooks and equipment in a plastic storage box with a lid. On days they are due to move to their other home, the whole box can move with them, and they will always have what they need.

SHOULD YOU GET YOUR CHILD A THERAPIST

Give it time

As mentioned earlier, children are likely to experience significant effects from the breakup, particularly in the short term. However, many of their emotions and behaviors can be considered normal during this period.

In younger children, these may include:

- Overly dependent attachment.
- Changes to sleep/nap routines.
- Relapse (for example, "forgetting" skills they have learnt, such as potty training).
- Anger, emotional outbreaks, and/or aggression.

- Self-blame.
- Crying.
- Continually asking for the other parent.

In older children and teens, these may include:

- Anger and emotional outbreaks.
- Withdrawal from friends and activities.
- Self-blame.
- Becoming concerned about adult problems, such as finances.

Remember that time is a great healer—in many cases, with your help and reassurance, children will settle into their new situations and routines and will be absolutely fine. Sometimes all children really need is your love and patience, and in those circumstances, pushing therapy onto them could actually be counterproductive.

Warning signs

However, there are some behaviors that may indicate your child is struggling to cope with the divorce.

In younger children, these warning signs include:

- Excessive worry or anxiety.
- Difficulty separating from you.
- Persistent eating problems, such as refusing food.
- Complaints of physical symptoms such as stomachaches or headaches.
- Persistent nightmares or insomnia.

- Persistently disruptive or aggressive behavior, particularly harming other children.

In older children and teens, these warning signs include:

- Dishonest behavior, such as lying or stealing.
- A decline in academic performance.
- Changes in peer groups or relationships with friends.
- Loss of interest in previously enjoyed activities.
- Substance misuse, including drugs, alcohol etc.
- Hypersexuality.
- Aggressive and/or antisocial or criminal behavior.
- Obsessive compulsiveness.
- Insomnia and/or difficulty focusing or concentrating.
- Persistent chronic fatigue or lethargy.
- Being extremely uncommunicative.

If you're seeing any of these behaviors, it might be time to seek professional support. Therapists can work directly with the child and/or with the whole family. They will help everyone find ways to process what is going on, deal with change and feelings of sadness and guilt, and improve communication.

The narcissist factor

Let's not forget that you are battling other factors, namely an uncooperative and narcissistic ex. If both parents are not on the same page, the messages your children receive may be overshadowed by the conflict. Even if you're not seeing any troubling behaviors from your children, you might want to consider a counselor's help if your ex is making your separation particularly challenging. A counselor will serve as a neutral third party and will be able to will help to protect your child from any negative, narcissistic influences. They will also be able to help spot any more serious abuse.

HOW TO KNOW IF THE NARCISSIST IS ABUSING YOUR CHILD

Recap of narcissistic personality traits

Let's quickly recap the narcissistic behaviors you learnt to recognize in Chapter One. They may include:

- Excessive self-importance and entitlement.
- Excessive craving for admiration and validation.
- Extreme sensitivity to criticism.
- Using manipulation and exploitation for personal gain or satisfaction.
- Lacking empathy and disregarding others.

You are probably well accustomed to many of these behaviors. But how does this apply to children? What kind of parents do narcissists make? And what separates abuse from typical narcissistic behaviors?

Understanding narcissistic abuse

Narcissistic abuse is a unique form of abuse, as it originates from the narcissist's personality traits and ingrained patterns of behavior. Their need for admiration, sense of entitlement, and lack of empathy can all potentially contribute to abusive behaviors. However, it's important to note that not all narcissists are abusive, and not all abusive individuals are narcissists.

Abuse occurs when narcissists engage in manipulative and harmful behaviors that cause emotional, psychological, or even physical harm to others. Types of abuse highly associated with narcissism include:

- **Emotional abuse**—Narcissists may belittle, criticize, or manipulate other people to maintain a sense of superiority and control.
- **Verbal abuse**—Insults, name-calling, and harsh language may be used to demean and control others.
- **Psychological abuse**—Narcissists may engage in gaslighting, which involves undermining a person's reality by denying facts, experiences, or feelings.
- **Financial abuse**—Narcissists may control other people by restricting their access to financial resources, making it difficult for them to leave or become independent.

Regardless of the intensity of their traits, people with narcissistic tendencies frequently exploit their children to fulfill their need for narcissistic supply. Children can be perceived as vulnerable and defenseless, making them ideal targets for narcissistic abuse. This is because they do not possess the necessary skills or knowledge to defend themselves against such harmful behaviors.

Narcissistic abuse could result in various outcomes, depending on what predominant type of narcissist the parent is (Lo, 2022).

Predominant categorizations of narcissistic parents and their impact on children

- Competitive narcissists are considered highly jealous of their children and any attention they receive. They often want to be the center of attention and may do whatever they can to make sure the focus is on them. They will often copy the activities and interests of the child, trying to outdo them. They will withhold their approval and affection if they are displeased and can also launch into fits of rage if they feel their child is somehow better at these activities than them. This may cause children to learn to hide or downplay their achievements. They can grow up feeling guilty for being successful and can self-sabotage in later life.

- Dismissive narcissists may fear intimacy and find it difficult to connect with others. They can be scared that their children might start to matter to them, and for this reason, they may push them away. They can be distant and cold towards their children, show no interest in their activities, and can be dismissive of their emotions. They often find reasons to be busy or away from home and overcompensate with expensive gifts. Children grow up doubting their own self-worth and lacking in confidence.
- Grandiose narcissists are extremely self-important. Their children may be expected to continually give them excessive adoration, or they may feel pressure to achieve praise so that their parent can accept it as their own. These narcissists may only show affection if their children please them. They tend to push their children to overachieve and will be abusive if their expectations are not met. Children may grow up with a fear of failure and often become overachieving perfectionists.
- Enmeshed narcissists are fragile and insecure. They may depend on their children to supply the reassurance and love that they didn't receive themselves. They tend to make everything about them and will interfere in their children's lives to make the child feel they cannot

manage without their parents. In consequence, children may feel forced to put their parents first and struggle to become independent in later life.

Abuse risk factors

Several risk factors may increase the likelihood of your child experiencing narcissistic abuse. Be extra vigilant if these apply to your situation. They may include:

- **Severe narcissistic traits**—If the narcissistic parent has more predominant narcissistic traits or is diagnosed with NPD, they are more prone to become abusive.
- **History of abusive behavior**—If the narcissistic parent has a history of abusive behavior towards you or others.
- **High-conflict divorce or separation**—A high-conflict divorce or separation can exacerbate the narcissistic parent's abusive tendencies.
- **Isolation**—If the narcissistic parent isolates the child from friends, family, or other support networks, it may increase the likelihood of abuse.
- **Substance abuse**—If the narcissistic parent struggles with substance abuse, it may increase the risk of abuse towards the child.
- **Other mental health concerns**—The presence of certain additional mental health issues in the narcissistic parent can further increase the likelihood of abusive behavior.

Signs of abuse

It may be easy to recognize abuse when it's happening to you, but knowing what signs to look for in your child may be less straightforward. Still, it is important, especially because you can't always be by their side. So what can you do to determine if your child is experiencing abuse? A lot of it will be about listening to your child. Are they doing or expressing anything that might raise a concern? For instance, do they:

- Have difficulty forming or maintaining friendships?
- Show sudden changes in academic performance or school attendance?
- Question the love or affection of their narcissistic parent?
- Constantly seek the reassurance of your love and support?
- Experience self-doubt and struggle with self-confidence?
- Express feelings of being unlovable or no good?
- Worry that they might say or do the wrong thing?
- Flinch or become fearful when voices are raised or during arguments?
- Put a great deal of pressure on themselves and/or get angry with themselves when they fail to win or succeed?
- Report a lack of respect for their privacy from their other parent?
- Voice excessive jealousy of their sibling or tell you that they get told off for things their brother or sister does not?
- Display regressive behaviors, such as bed-wetting or thumb-sucking?
- Regularly assume blame, even when it's not their responsibility?
- Avoid confrontation with siblings, often giving in to their demands?
- Show little interest in extracurricular activities or never talk about their interests?

- Express excessive worry about adult issues or concerns beyond their age?

Indeed, some of these behaviors are normal aspects of childhood development, and not every issue is necessarily indicative of narcissistic abuse. Children have unique personalities; some may naturally be more introverted or accommodating than others. However, as a parent who knows your child well, you should trust your instincts and be attentive to any major changes in their behavior, emotions, or interactions with the narcissistic parent. If you notice patterns that concern you or if your child shares information about their experiences in the other parent's household that raises red flags, it's essential to take these signs seriously and consider the possibility of narcissistic abuse. Addressing the issue early can help protect your child's emotional and mental well-being and prevent further harm.

However, the following signs should be considered more alarming and warrant immediate attention. Does your child:

- Appear emotionally numb, detached, or socially withdrawn?
- Show signs of depression or anxiety?
- Show signs of self-harm or suicidal thoughts?
- Have unexplained injuries, such as bruises, cuts, or burns?
- Display drastic changes in eating habits, such as a loss of appetite or binge eating?
- Experience extreme mood swings or emotional outbursts?
- Have persistent nightmares or insomnia?

- Fear or avoid the narcissistic parent?

Should you observe any of these heightened warning signs in your child or come across any more direct indications of abuse, it's imperative to take the following steps:

1. **Immediately prioritize your child's safety**—Remove them from potentially dangerous situations and ensure they are in a safe and supportive environment.
2. **Report the abuse**—Depending on the severity of the situation, you may need to report the abuse to your local child protective services agency or law enforcement. They can assess the situation and take appropriate action to protect your child.
3. **Seek professional help**—Consult with a mental health professional, such as a psychologist or therapist, who has experience dealing with abuse and trauma.
4. **Document the abuse**—Keep detailed records of any incidents, including photos of injuries, dates, times, and descriptions of events. This information can be crucial if legal action is necessary later.
5. **Get legal advice**—Consult with a family law attorney who can help you navigate the legal system and advise you on the best course of action, such as modifying custody arrangements or obtaining a restraining order. More on this later in Chapter Eight.
6. **Offer emotional support**—Be there for your child, listen to their feelings and concerns, and reassure them that they are loved and cared for. Help them rebuild their sense of self-worth and security.

SUMMARY

Divorce and separation can have a massive impact on children both in the short term and the long term. When dealing with a narcissistic ex-partner, supporting your child during this period is critical. By remaining calm, honest, loving, and reassuring, you can help your child adjust to the separation and minimize the potential harm caused by the narcissistic behavior of their other parent.

Children may experience a range of emotions after parental separation, including sadness, anger, and confusion. While you can't eliminate these feelings, you can offer guidance and support as they navigate this new reality. Remember that, just like you, children need time and space to adjust to the changes happening in their lives.

As time passes, most families will adapt to the new situation. However, do keep a look out for any particularly troubling behavior which is very uncharacteristic for your children and/or which is not improving over time. Unfortunately, children can be vulnerable targets for narcissists, and they may experience various forms of abuse. It's essential to be vigilant and monitor your child for any unusual behaviors or signs that your ex-partner may be negatively affecting them. If you suspect that your child is being impacted by your ex's narcissistic behavior, consult with a therapist to ensure their well-being.

Action items

- Write down the techniques you are going to implement from this chapter to further help your child adjust to the separation.

- Observe and understand your child's emotions and behaviors. Use this behavior as a healthy baseline to better notice warning signs in the future and take note of any warning signs.
- If some warning signs are present, consider seeking professional support from a therapist or counselor for your child. If the more serious signs are present, take *immediate* action to prioritize your child's safety, then follow the steps detailed at the end of this chapter.

CHAPTER 5
HOW TO BE THE HEALTHY PARENT YOUR CHILD NEEDS

As you saw in Chapter Three, your child may have some considerable challenges to face as they grow up with a narcissistic parent. It's up to you to be the healthy, balanced parent who is going to help them survive and thrive. You need to teach them healthy behaviors. You need to ensure they are strong enough to withstand whatever your ex deals out. Let's have a look at how to make that happen.

OVERCOMING THE IMPACT OF NARCISSISTIC RELATIONSHIPS

Young children are highly observant and tend to learn more through imitation rather than verbal instruction. They pay close attention to the people around them and mimic the behaviors they see, which often have more influence than what you explicitly teach or tell them. That's why it's important for you to set a good example—by showing them healthy and positive actions.

Analogically, you wouldn't want to hire a personal trainer who looks as though they couldn't even run for a bus and who lives off fried food and buckets of soda. You want to hire someone who is in really great shape and who demonstrates the behaviors you need to look and feel amazing as well.

Just as you would want a personal trainer who embodies a healthy lifestyle, you need to be in a good mental and emotional state to support your child.

Building on the techniques Chapter One presented, which focused on building resilience, this chapter will expand on them to provide a more in-depth understanding of how to not only just cope with challenges but also how to actively overcome them.

Seeking professional help

To effectively guide your child, it's essential to address any lingering issues from your past relationship with the narcissistic parent. Regardless of the duration of your relationship with your ex, their behavior likely affected your mental and emotional well-being. You may have experienced a range of challenging behaviors, such as constant criticism, threats, silent treatment, deceit, manipulation, and attempts to sabotage your relationships or activities.

Previous chapters discussed how these behaviors can affect your child. But what about you? The aftermath of such abuse can manifest in various ways, such as self-blame, anxiety, reduced confidence, negative thoughts, or lingering guilt for leaving the relationship.

Narcissistic abuse syndrome is a term used by mental health professionals and survivors to describe this cluster of symptoms that can arise in such situation. It is not an officially recognized mental health diagnosis, but narcissistic abuse syndrome includes symptoms that are similar to Post-Traumatic Stress Disorder (PTSD). So don't underestimate the impact that a narcissist can have on you. If you are suffering from anxiety, depression, or self-harming behaviors or cannot move past your feelings of negativity, seek professional help.

Here are some tips and questions to consider when searching for a therapist:

- **Credentials**—Ensure that the therapist is licensed and has the appropriate education and training in their field (e.g., they are a qualified psychologist, psychiatrist, social worker, or counselor).
- **Approach**—Therapists use various therapeutic approaches, such as cognitive behavioral therapy, psychodynamic therapy, or humanistic therapy. Find out which approach they use and if it aligns with your needs and preferences.
- **Experience**—Ask how long they have been practicing and if they have experience working with clients who have faced challenges like yours, such as co-parenting with a narcissistic ex or similar personality disorders.
- **Availability**—Find out if they have openings and if their schedule matches yours. Also, ask about the frequency and duration of sessions.
- **Fees and insurance**—Ask about the cost of therapy sessions, payment options, and if they accept your health insurance.
- **Personal fit**—It's important to feel comfortable with your therapist. You may want to schedule an initial

consultation or phone call to gauge whether you feel a good rapport with them.

Remember, it may take some extra effort to find the therapist suited to your needs, but it will be worth it for a successful experience, and it saves you time switching later on.

Reframe your negative thoughts—Challenge that headline

Chapter One discussed the importance of having a positive mindset as a foundation for resilience. Now, you're going to learn more about that concept and explore how to actively reframe your negative thoughts, like those that may arise from dealing with your ex. The "challenge that headline" technique is a practical and effective method for transforming negative self-talk into a more balanced perspective, providing a powerful example for your child to follow.

The technique can be applied as follows. Pretend that the voice in your head is a sensationalist news reporter whose best interest is to exaggerate everything. Their wild exaggerations are a reminder that you can't believe everything that you hear because there is always another side to any story. For example, let's say that you forgot to set your alarm and were late dropping the children off at school. The voice in your head might conjure up the headline "Worst Mom (or Dad) in the world is late again!" or "Total waste of space can't get anything right!" That kind of talk is very easy to listen to, and worse, it will cement those negative thought patterns, so you are more likely to look for the worst in your own behavior the next time around.

Instead, let's interview those who were involved.

Reporter: Did you forget to set the alarm?

You: Yes.

Reporter: When was the last time you forgot?

You: I don't actually remember.

Reporter: So it isn't a frequent occurrence?

You: No.

Reporter: Why do you think it happened this time?

You: Because I was up late last night doing some extra work.

Reporter: And why were you doing extra work?

You: Because I wanted to earn some extra money for the children.

Reporter: Does that sound like something the worst parent in the world would do?

You: Nope.

You get the idea. Hear the big headline that your negativity comes up with and give yourself an honest interview to see what is really going on. By challenging your negative thoughts and reframing them in a more balanced light, you can improve your self-perception and reduce the impact of negative self-talk. If you find it difficult to think of positive aspects of yourself, mentally interview your Mom or a close friend. What would they say about the situation? Would they tell you that you are the worst Mom in the world? Probably not.

Embrace the *and* mindset

Up to this point, your controlling, narcissistic ex has likely had a significant influence on your life. When you were together, you probably found yourself changing your behavior to suit them—doing or not doing things to keep them satisfied. However, you need to remember that you're no longer together. They may still be in your life because of the children, and they might continue to create difficulties. But now, they are just an element of your life, not the defining feature. They can no longer dictate your every move.

Consider this analogy: You wouldn't let an unreasonable work colleague dictate your personal interests, like taking up ballroom dancing, learning Spanish, or reading more. Your colleague might be a nightmare to work with, but what you do outside of work is none of their business. Yes, they might try and impose on your time or get you to go to work on your day off. They might be unproductive, meaning you have to pick up all the slack. This might make it *difficult* to find the time to do the things you want to do, but it does not control you. Think about your ex in the same light. They are someone you have to cooperate with for the sake of your children. They might be a challenging "colleague," but they can't control your personal life.

Adopting this mindset will help you to reframe your thoughts from *but* to *and*. Think, "I want to take up ballroom dancing *and* I have an unreasonable ex," instead of "I want to take up ballroom dancing *but* I have an unreasonable ex." The first part of your life is not dependent on the second. Don't give your ex any more control over you! They can't command your life anymore, so live it the way you want to.

CHALLENGE YOUR UNHEALTHY HABITS

As mentioned earlier, children will mimic your behaviors. For children, imitation is primarily an unconscious process. They naturally observe and absorb the behaviors of those around them, especially their parents, without consciously realizing they are doing so. As they grow and develop, they may begin to consciously imitate certain behaviors, but much of the learning still occurs unconsciously. Imitation is a basic learning mechanism that allows them to understand their social environment, acquire new skills, and embrace the standards and values of their family and culture.

With this in mind, it's easy to understand why you should avoid swearing or smoking around your children. However, other habits may not be as apparent, and you might not even realize you're doing them. Examples include being overly critical of yourself, focusing on your children's negative behaviors, procrastinating, or gossiping. Just as your children may learn to smoke by watching you, they may also adopt these other habits.

Breaking unhealthy habits can be challenging, as they form neural pathways in the brain. Remember the ski slope analogy? That applies to your behaviors and habits, too, because breaking an unhealthy habit requires deliberate action and effort to get out of those tracks, just as correcting negative thoughts does.

For example, let's say that you want to stop using self-deprecating language. You have realized that it is an unhealthy habit, which is great. Next, just notice every time you are doing it. You don't need to do anything else at this point—just bring it to your awareness. In the same way as creating a budget makes you very aware of your spending, taking note of a habit is the first step in changing it. For example, every time you catch yourself talking in a self-critical way, step back and take a mental note.

Next, remind yourself of why you need to change the habit. You know that if the children hear you putting yourself down, they could start to become overly critical of themselves. You don't want them growing up feeling that they aren't good enough. If you want them to have self-confidence, you are going to have to start modelling that for them.

Figure out your triggers and see if you can remove them. Is there anything in particular that causes you to feel bad about yourself? Perhaps you read lots of magazines that only show "perfect" models who make you feel ugly? Get rid of them. Do your friends put themselves down all the time? Maybe you should find s more positive people to surround yourself with. Or bring them on board with breaking the habit together?

Next, see if you can replace the habit with something else. In this case, every time you want to say something negative about yourself, try saying something positive instead. It can be hard, and it will feel unnatural for a while, but over time, you will rewire those neural pathways, and the positive thoughts will come far more naturally.

Change is hard. It won't happen overnight. To break a habit, you really have to be consistent and patient. Be kind to yourself. If you slip up, don't give up—just keep trying. Over time, it will become easier, and your children will benefit from your positive example.

RESIST USING YOUR CHILD

One thing that your children won't thank you for is putting them in the middle of your squabbles with your ex.

Your ex might stoop to bad-mouthing you to your children. They might tell the children that you don't pay your share. They might try to argue with you in their presence. They may make the children feel guilty for their time spent with you. While you can't control your ex's actions, you can model the right way to handle conflict by rising above these behaviors.

Bad-mouthing your ex in retaliation to your children is unfair to them and will not achieve anything good. Remember that your ex is their other parent, and you owe it to your children to have the opportunity to love that parent. Do not speak badly of them in any way, either to the children themselves or to other people in front of them. This also includes showing disdain or complete disinterest in what the children have to say about your ex. You might not want to hear it, but be glad that they are happy and that they want to share their news with you.

As mentioned in Chapter Two, don't fight with your ex. Not only because it adds fuel to their narcissistic fire but also because it is uncomfortable and upsetting for your children to have to witness it. They might see your ex being mean and trying to fight with you, but if they see you not engaging and remaining calm and respectful, they might appreciate you for it. Try to remember that you are supposed to be working together as a team for your children's well-being and that fighting with the other member of the team will get you nowhere. Instead, keep your eyes on the prize—your children's well-being.

Keep your children out of any communication between you and your ex. This might be tempting; after all, you are trying to limit the amount of contact you have with the ex. But asking your children to pass messages back and forth only puts them in the middle and adds unnecessary stress to their lives. It isn't their job to communicate with your ex—it is yours.

Don't make your children feel guilty for spending time away from you. Allow them to enjoy their time with the other parent without burdening them with excessive calls or expressing how much you miss them. Although well intended, these actions could make your children think that you are lonely or sad without them, and that, in turn, may make them feel responsible for your feelings. It's fine to give them a call if they are away for a lengthy period, but don't call them every day or make them feel bad for not calling you. It's generally best to just let them enjoy their time with their other parent and to try to show genuine interest in what they have been up to when they get back (without prying too much for details).

Remember, it is not their choice to have to go between two homes, so make it as easy for them as you can. Ultimately, your main focus should be to create a supportive environment that allows your children to feel happy and secure, regardless of which parent they are with. By granting them the freedom to have their own relationships and experiences, you provide them with a valuable gift in the aftermath of family separation.

PROMOTING COMMUNICATION WITH YOUR CHILD

Children face numerous challenges as they grow and develop. As well as all the pressures of school, they are trying to learn who they are, where they fit in, what's right and what's wrong, and how the world works. As they grow, they have to navigate puberty, relationships, increased responsibility, money management, and have to try and figure out what they want to do in the future. In addition to these, your children must also cope with living in two different homes and dealing with a difficult parent. To support them through these obstacles, it's vital to establish and maintain open communication with them.

Without healthy communication habits with your children, they may struggle to reach out to you. As they reach their teenage years, if they don't know how to talk to you, they most likely won't. A lack of communication can lead to the buildup of unresolved issues and emotional turmoil. Your children need a level-headed, understanding, and approachable adult they can turn to when they need help or guidance.

To keep the lines of communication open, ensure your children know they can talk to you about anything at any time. While some of their concerns may be unfamiliar or different from your own experiences, simply being a supportive listener can make a big difference. Your love and support will provide them with the comfort and reassurance they need to face life's challenges.

So how do you prioritize communication? How do you get to the point where your child feels comfortable coming to you for help and support?

Make time for meaningful conversation

It often goes as follows. Your children are trying to tell you something. You're trying to make dinner, feed the dog, put the washing on, clean the bathroom, or whatever. You're also trying to think about what you need to do tomorrow or what your Mom said yesterday. In your busy life, it's easy to find yourself only half-listening to your children as you juggle various tasks and responsibilities. You throw out a "That's nice, sweetie!" or "Great!" and hope that they will stop chattering soon and leave you in peace.

Everyone is busy. Being "busy" is a common perception, as people from all walks of life tend to view themselves as occupied, regardless of their specific roles and responsibilities.

Despite the seemingly constant state of busyness, it's crucial to prioritize and carve out dedicated time for your children. When your child is little, they probably won't notice that you aren't always really listening. But as they get older, they will. You could be missing something really significant, and your child may then be upset because they thought they told you about it. They'll soon realize when you aren't paying attention, and they may stop bothering you.

To avoid this, let your child know that you genuinely want to hear what they have to say, but you need to complete your task first. Once you're finished, give them your undivided attention, and engage in a thoughtful conversation.

Setting aside regular, individual time for each child to chat without distractions can help strengthen your bond and encourage open communication. Bedtime can be a great opportunity for these conversations, as it offers a calm and intimate environment. Though the discussions may be lighthearted, your child will know they have a designated time to share their thoughts and concerns.

Additionally, make mealtimes a priority for family conversation. Research has shown that shared meals contribute to better emotional and mental health and improved academic performance for children (Hammons & Fiese, 2011). While it can be difficult to get everyone together daily, aim for a few times a week, be it breakfast or dinner. These moments provide an excellent opportunity for connection, encouraging a supportive and communicative family atmosphere.

Active listening in parenting

When you listen to music, audiobooks, or podcasts, your engagement is passive. You hear the content, but no response is required. Sure, you might sing along or laugh, but you could just as easily sit in silence. It doesn't make any difference to the recording.

However, when conversing with someone, especially your children, active listening is crucial. To show them that you're listening and understanding, use nonverbal cues like nodding or smiling and verbal cues like "Uh-huh" or "Right." To enhance your listening even further, ask questions, voice opinions, and show your interest. Even if the topic isn't your favorite, it's essential to demonstrate that you're trying. Even if you've lost count of the number of hours you've listened to your son talking about soccer, which you know very little about. But let him see you are making an effort.

It's a good idea to ask specific questions rather than general ones. If you ask your son what he did in school that day, he will invariably say, "Stuff." If you ask him what the best thing was he did in school that day, you'll get much more input. Children love to tell you their favorites and least favorites, and they love lists too, so "Tell me your top five (of anything)" is usually a winner. Inquire about their friends, the books they're reading, or the games they're playing. Ensure your questions can't be answered with a simple yes or no.

Additionally, refrain from judging your children's interests. It's ok to admit that you don't know much about a particular topic or that it isn't your favorite, but avoid devaluing their interests. Criticizing their preferences may discourage them from sharing in the future. As children grow, they might make mistakes or ignore your advice. However, if you judge them, they may stop seeking your guidance altogether.

Open communication

To encourage your children to feel comfortable talking to you, lead by example and engage in conversations with them. Demonstrating openness and honesty in your discussions can inspire them to do the same.

Of course, it's important to speak to them at an age-appropriate level. While you might be interested in complex topics, remember to choose subjects that will resonate with your child. Just talk about something general that interests you or your likes and dislikes. When my son was six, he started asking me for a memory of my childhood every night; this tradition continued for years and was great fuel for conversation. You could also talk about what's going on in the world. For younger children, chat about what you can see in the neighborhood. For older children, you could discuss current events or news stories.

One thing you shouldn't discuss, however, is adult problems that are beyond a child's understanding or ability to cope with. While it is essential to teach children empathy and emotional awareness, sharing adult problems with them can be overwhelming and may lead to feelings of anxiety, stress, or responsibility that they are not yet equipped to manage. It is essential for parents to strike a balance between teaching emotional intelligence and protecting their children from undue emotional burden. Remember, they have plenty to deal with in their own lives, so focus on supporting them and maintaining open communication.

INTRODUCING THE CONCEPT OF NARCISSISM

While discussing the importance of maintaining open and honest communication with your child, you might wonder if you should teach them about narcissists. Should you explain your ex's behavior? Wouldn't that make it easier for your children to handle things? Well, the answer is both yes and no.

Remember what you learnt about not bad-mouthing their other parent? That principle also applies to telling them that their Mom or Dad is a raging narcissist. They want to be free to love their parent, so this information can only be negative. Not only might it make them uncomfortable and wary around your ex, but they might also resent you.

However, if left to their own devices, one of two things will happen. Either they will grow up being very attuned to narcissistic behavior—able to spot it a mile away and unwilling to tolerate it—or they will become used to it, accepting it as the norm. They may be subconsciously drawn to it in future relationships, and so used to suppressing their own needs that they continue to do so as an adult.

So, what's the solution? The best thing to do is teach them about narcissism in general terms without relating it to your ex. This will help them become aware of unhealthy behaviors, recognize what is unacceptable, and ultimately, shield themselves from it. They will probably piece things together for themselves later, but for now, don't jump the gun and tell them that you're talking about their Mom or Dad.

In sum, model good behaviors. Teach them that it's beneficial to be positive, empathetic, and forgiving, but they also need to look after themselves. Set boundaries in your own house and stick to them. You can also help them indirectly by showing them that you are indifferent to your ex's behavior. Rise above it; pretend it doesn't affect you in the slightest. This may help teach your child that they don't need to be affected by name-calling and belittling. You are better than that, and so are they.

HELP YOUR CHILD LEARN SKILLS FOR SURVIVING AND THRIVING AS AN ADULT

The job description of a parent seems incredibly long and complex. There are just so many tasks you are expected to handle—picking up, dropping off, cooking, helping with homework, playing games, nurturing friendships, and bandaging scraped knees, to name a few.

However, these are just the day-to-day tasks. What is the purpose of the job? What is the end goal? Essentially, you are responsible for equipping your children with the skills they need to grow into capable, competent adults.

Of course, some of these skills are practical. It's crucial to teach your children how to cook, manage their time and money, and maintain a household. But beyond these basics, what else should you be teaching your children so that they not only survive but also thrive as adults?

Responsibility and perseverance

When children go through tough times like divorce or separation, they often learn about responsibility and sticking to things without even realizing it. These experiences can teach them important life lessons and help them become stronger, especially if parents are there to support them. But you can still take additional steps to actively reinforce these skills.

Encourage your child to own their choices and learn from any mistakes they make. Give them tasks that fit their age, like doing chores or keeping up with their homework. This way, they'll learn to commit to things and understand how important it is to follow through on what they've promised.

Make sure your child knows that challenges and setbacks happen to everyone and that never giving up is the key to overcoming problems and succeeding in life. Share stories from your life or about famous people who have shown strength and determination in tough situations. Keep encouraging your child to keep going, even when things are hard, and celebrate their hard work and accomplishments.

Social skills

Sure, your children would *survive* without great social skills. Your ex managed it, didn't they?! But the question remains—will they truly thrive? Will they be capable of forming happy, successful relationships? Will they secure their desired positions at work? If they are rude and inconsiderate, the odds may not be in their favor. You must teach them basic manners but also how to function in society—how to cooperate and compromise and how to forgive (themselves as well as others)? How to admit their mistakes and say sorry? How to understand other people's feelings? How to communicate effectively? And how to share? One crucial aspect of this, which you have already covered, is empathy.

So how do you go about teaching the rest of these social skills? It's very simple. Just like empathy, model them yourself. Demonstrate good manners by saying please and thank you in public, offering your seat to the elderly on the bus, and showing consideration for others. Compromise with your children—for example, if they don't want to eat all their peas, suggest they eat half. Apologize when you make a mistake and express love and support even after they've misbehaved. By observing your actions, they will naturally adopt these positive behaviors.

Encourage your children to stick up for themselves and voice what they want. One of my sons is very easygoing and laid back; the other is very assertive and determined. I continually have to encourage the former to voice his opinion and to stick up for what he wants instead of always submitting to his brother. In his mind, he is being nice or doesn't really mind, so he is happy for his brother to get his own way. And sometimes that is fine. But I have to be careful he doesn't fall into the habit of becoming a people pleaser. If he never acknowledges his own needs, he will end up with people taking advantage of his good nature. So work to find ways to ensure that everyone gets a say. When each child feels their voice counts, and there isn't always one person dominating, they'll be more likely to speak up in the future.

Critical thinking and decision-making

While schools play a role in teaching children how to think, it's also the parents' responsibility to support their child's intellectual development. Schools provide some of the knowledge needed to succeed in the world, but parents can help by promoting curiosity, independent learning, focus, critical thinking, and decision-making skills.

Cultivating curiosity in a child is crucial for their success in school and beyond. Curious children approach the world with an open mind, embrace new experiences and challenges, and continuously learn and grow. Encourage curiosity by pointing out interesting things on walks, in books, or while watching TV, and prompt your child to do the same. Ask your child questions, and if neither of you knows the answer, take the time to brainstorm possible solutions, no matter how outlandish they may be. This approach encourages imagination and creativity. Once you've both shared your ideas, search for the actual answers together. Expose your child to the fascinating aspects of the world to help them appreciate its wonders.

Teaching your child critical thinking is super important too. To do well as grown-ups, they need to be able to think deeper and come up with their own ideas. The world needs people who look for answers to tough questions and don't just believe everything they hear. Studies have shown that being a good critical thinker and decision-maker can lead to success in many areas of life (Dwyer et al., 2014).

Encourage critical thinking by getting your children to solve problems; give them some fun challenges and see what solutions they can come up with. Play board games or video games with puzzles or problem-solving elements. Discuss your decision-making processes with them and support them in making their own choices. If they receive an allowance, help them decide how to manage their money responsibly. Activities that require considering options and evaluating different choices will strengthen their critical thinking and decision-making abilities.

Helping children make choices is simpler when they know what is important to them. Talk with them about what they care about and how they want to use their time and energy. This self-awareness will enable them to make decisions that align with their own well-being.

Focus and delayed gratification

In an age with unprecedented access to information, parents need to do more than just teach their children basic skills. You also have to show them the right way to use things like smartphones and the internet appropriately. As parents, you need to get used to this new reality and help your children learn how to handle a connected and fast-changing world.

It's more important than ever to teach children about the value of waiting for things they want and being able to focus even when there are many distractions around. Both of these skills require people to avoid distractions and say no to things they want right away so they can reach bigger and more important goals later on. The marshmallow test is a famous experiment that looked at how well children can wait for something they want. In the test, a child could pick one marshmallow right away or wait for a bigger reward of more marshmallows later. The study found that children who were able to wait and delay gratification had better outcomes later in areas such as academic achievement, health, and social skills (Mischel et al., 1989). Today, it's even harder for children to learn these skills because of distractions from digital devices, on top of the usual real-life distractions around them, like noisy classmates.

When you talk about using digital devices, it's important to know that not all screen time is the same. Watching a movie with the family is different from using a smartphone or tablet because of how it holds your attention.

During a family movie night, everyone is focused on the same thing. This kind of screen time is about enjoying something together and feeling closer to each other. On the flip side, using smartphones or tablets usually means looking at lots of short videos or playing easy games. This constant quick hopping from one task to another is called rapid context switching. Long periods spent on rapid context switching can lead to scattered attention, trouble focusing, and even stress (Rideout et al., 2010).

So, parents need to know the difference between the two kinds of screen time and find the right balance for their children. This way, it won't get in the way of study, sleep, exercise, and other important activities (AAP, 2016). Besides setting limits on screen time, parents should encourage their children to do things away from screens, like playing outside, reading, or other hobbies. This helps them grow in a balanced way, and they can retain their ability to focus.

Enjoyment

If you can teach your children to look after themselves, focus and navigate the complicated world of relationships, and be curious and critical in their thinking, you will have done a good job. However, there is one more essential skill that will contribute to their flourishing as adults: enjoyment.

You want your children to see the fun and enjoyment in life so that when they are adults, they can appreciate that not everything is about work and chores. At the end of the day, if you're not enjoying life, you're not truly thriving.

Find reasons to laugh with them. Make goofy faces, watch amusing videos, or simply laugh at lighthearted things. Dance around the kitchen and compete to create the most ridiculous dance moves. Most importantly, encourage them to laugh at themselves. People who don't take themselves too seriously are more likely to find humor in various situations and may not dwell on their failures. Gently poke fun at yourself to show them how to embrace their quirks.

Additionally, teach them to enjoy the process of trying. If you can instill in them the joy of new experiences, it is likely they won't avoid new opportunities. If you can teach them to appreciate a challenge and push themselves further, they'll probably strive for greater achievements as adults. Introduce them to new experiences and give them a chance to try novel things. Praise them for attempting something new and for not giving up. And embrace new experiences yourself. While it may be intimidating to face that waterslide or join a new class because seeing you take on challenges will help inspire them to do the same.

SUMMARY

There's no denying it: if you want to help your child overcome the negative effects of having a narcissistic parent, you need to put in some effort. On the most essential level, it's essential for you to be in the best possible shape to guide them effectively. So address any lingering issues from your past relationship. Examine how you approach challenges. Are you facing them head-on with a can-do attitude, or are you still using your ex as an excuse not to move forward in life? Consider your behaviors —are any of them unhealthy? Are you setting a positive example for your children? Answering these questions honestly will help you work diligently to demonstrate healthy behaviors and, as a result, will help your children develop good habits themselves.

And remember, don't let your child get caught in the middle when dealing with your ex. Aim to cooperate with their other parent, not work against them. Despite the challenges, you're ultimately on the same team.

Maintaining an honest communication line with your children will help them build skills essential in their adult life and deal with the potential impact of a narcissistic parent. So spend time discovering ways to communicate with your children and ensure they feel comfortable talking to you at any time. Dedicate moments to providing them with undivided attention. Listen actively, ask plenty of questions, and demonstrate genuine interest. Share details about your day and interests. By establishing strong communication with your child, you create an open door for them to approach you with any future problems.

Busy parents may often focus on ensuring the children's basic needs are met—providing food, warmth, and education. But what can you do to help them truly thrive? You can help them enhance their social skills so they become polite and considerate while also learning to assert themselves. You can foster curiosity, critical thinking, and focus. And you can guide them to find enjoyment in life and the world around them.

When one parent is narcissistic, it becomes even more important for you to teach these valuable skills to your child. The narcissistic parent's model behavior and advice may not be as good. By stepping up and making sure your child learns these important life skills, you can help them be ready for a successful and happy future, even if things are tough with their other parent.

Action items

- Make a list of any unresolved feelings or issues you have regarding your narcissistic ex and how these unhealthy behaviors might show up. Note down the steps you'll take to handle these situations better and set a positive example for your children.

- Aim to cooperate, not work against the other parent. Despite the challenges you face, ultimately, you are on the same team when it comes to the children. Ensure they do not get caught in the middle of you dealing with your ex.
- Set aside a consistent time for open communication with your children. Mealtimes or bedtime can be a great opportunity for these conversations. Dedicating to them your undivided attention, actively listening, asking questions, and demonstrating genuine interest will help your child to feel comfortable talking to you at any time.
- Help your child improve their social skills. Teach them to be polite and considerate while also asserting themselves. With your guidance, they can find enjoyment in their interactions with the people around them.
- Identify two skills you think your child would benefit from improving. Consider areas where they might not be as strong or won't likely learn from school or their narcissistic parent. Write down specific actions you'll take to help your child develop these skills.

CHAPTER 6
USING BOUNDARY SETTINGS TO KEEP THINGS ORDERLY

Previous chapters have touched on boundaries, but you may still be wondering exactly what the term means. What exactly are boundaries? Why are they important? How will they help me? And how do you set and maintain them?

WHAT ARE PERSONAL BOUNDARIES

Boundaries are simple to understand when applied to land and property. Your property ends at a certain point, and mine begins. One town could be in France, while the other is in Spain.

Consider your home and property. If someone were to break in and steal your possessions, it's expected that you'd feel angry and upset. If your neighbor consistently disposes of their garden waste on your property, you'd be unhappy. If a friend were to use your car without your permission, you'd probably be on the phone asking them what on earth they thought they were doing.

Personal boundaries function in a similar way. Your boundaries end where mine start. These are my needs, and those are yours. Your boundaries determine your identity, the behaviors you'll tolerate from others, and what others can anticipate from you. If someone violates those boundaries, you experience an emotional response, much like when someone intrudes on your land or property.

There are six different kinds of boundaries:

- **Physical**—respect for another's personal space and their comfort levels regarding touch.
- **Sexual**—respect for another's choices concerning sexual partners, activities, and timings.
- **Intellectual**—respect for another's ideas and opinions.
- **Emotional**—respect for another's feelings.
- **Material/Financial**—respect for another's property, money, and financial choices.
- **Temporal**—respect for another's time and how much they can commit to you.

In each of these categories, you set what you are willing and unwilling to accept. Healthy boundaries enable you to define your identity and desires, prevent others from exploiting you, maintain healthy relationships, and achieve balance in your life. When your boundaries are respected, you feel safe and valued. If they are not respected, you could end up feeling anxious, overwhelmed, and devalued.

WHAT DO HEALTHY AND UNHEALTHY BOUNDARIES LOOK LIKE

Throughout my work, I've assisted many people in overcoming the challenges of divorce, co-parenting, and rebuilding their self-worth. Often, they started off believing that their problems were solely due to their exes, who were unreasonable, abusive, or manipulative. While these factors were indeed true, I also had to help them understand that part of their problem was their own approach. For instance, if you don't establish healthy boundaries, you become vulnerable to being used, abused, and manipulated, essentially contributing to enabling these harmful situations. It is only when you begin setting healthy boundaries and adhering to them that you realize how much control you can regain in their lives.

Perhaps you have a hard time saying no to people. Imagine having a busy week at work, and your boss asks you to put in a few hours over the weekend as well. You already have many things to catch up on at home and want to spend time with the children, but you say yes anyway. Then, your neighbor asks you to help them on Saturday for a couple of hours, and you end up doing that, too. By Sunday, you're completely exhausted, feeling like you never have any time to rest. You're tired, overwhelmed, and stressed out. In this scenario, how you are feeling is a result of unhealthy boundaries and the inability to freely say no to things. You might be continually overcommitting your time to other people, and therefore, you may not be looking after yourself. This is like letting strangers wander around your house and garden whenever they feel like it. You wouldn’t let anyone come in and help themselves to your cereal and watch your TV. And even if they were a friend, they would usually be there at agreed-upon and limited amounts of time.

The same applies to your time, focus, and energy. To maintain them, you need a stronger fence. With healthy boundaries, you are better at prioritizing time for yourself. You strive to will help if you have the energy and the capacity but realize that you are not responsible for other people's problems. This way, you can ensure that when it's time to be there for others, such as for your children who depend on you, you'll be feeling rejuvenated rather than burnt out.

Perhaps you find yourself in one terrible relationship after another, seemingly attracting bullies who put you down and make you feel bad about yourself. Maybe they have cheated on you, or they've been very controlling about who you see and where you go. After a series of such relationships, you might start feeling undeserving of anything better. Unhealthy boundaries could be contributing to this because your behavior might appear as allowing others to treat you in ways that you don't deserve.

Imagine loaning someone your car. At first, they take care of it, but soon, they return it in a mess. There's trash everywhere, the paintwork is scratched, the engine has issues, and the radio is missing. You wouldn't be happy with that, right? So why do you let people treat you poorly? Why tolerate name-calling and cheating? It could be due to unhealthy boundaries. In contrast, if you establish healthy boundaries, you will be able more often stand up for yourself and refuse to accept mistreatment. You will develop a strong sense of self-respect and prioritize your need to feel safe and happy in a relationship.

Here's another example: your friends love skiing, and they plan a big trip every year. You can't really afford it, but they always persuade you to go. You'd feel guilty if you didn't go, and you worry about being left out if you don't participate. So you go, even though you don't enjoy skiing, and now you have no money left for things you actually want to do. Again, this is an example of unhealthy boundaries. Now imagine the same situation again, but this time you're honest with your friends about your feelings towards skiing and your financial concerns. You respectfully let them know that while you value the friendship and appreciate the invitation, you can't afford the trip, and skiing isn't your favorite activity. Instead, you propose a different, more affordable gathering or trip that everyone can enjoy together at a later date. You give your friends a chance to appreciate your honesty and understand your perspective. They may continue with their skiing plans, but they may also look forward to the alternative gathering you suggested. In this situation, you've established healthy boundaries without disrespecting your friends or devaluing your friendships. By expressing your needs and preferences clearly and politely, you will be better equipped to maintain strong relationships while staying true to yourself and your interests.

Imagine going to your favorite restaurant where you know exactly what you love to eat. But when you sit down to order, a friend insists on choosing your meal for you, selecting dishes you don't enjoy or can't afford. You probably wouldn't want to keep going to that restaurant with that friend, as it takes away the enjoyment of choosing your own meal and spending your money on what you truly want. Now imagine the same scenario, but this time, you confidently express your preferences and tell your friend that you'd like to choose your own meal.

You kindly let them know that you appreciate their suggestions, but you have your own taste and budget in mind. This approach will help your friend understand and respect your decision, and as a result, you both may enjoy your meals without any pressure or coercion. In this situation, you've established healthy boundaries with your friend.

Of course, everyone wants to be a good friend, good employee, good neighbor. I'm not saying that you should become completely self-centered and that you should only ever do what you want with no regard for anyone else. That would make you a narcissist! Having healthy boundaries isn't about being selfish. It's about balancing your own needs *as well* as those of others. Other people need your help or want your time, and it's absolutely fine to give it to them—as long as it is within your boundaries, which could mean considering the following questions: do you have the time? The capacity? Are you interested in that activity? Can you afford it? If yes, great, go ahead.

But if the answer (or answers) is no, and saying yes is going to make you feel uncomfortable, then you are well within your rights to say no. For instance, "I'm sorry. I really want to help you, but I don't have time." "I'm not really interested in skiing, and I can't afford it, but I'd love to hear about it when you get back." "I am not paid to work overtime, and I have other commitments." All of these are reasonable responses.

Now, let's consider boundaries in the context of relationships with your partner and closest family. Ask yourself if the way your partner, parent, or friend treats you is acceptable. Do they respect you? Value your opinions? Give you space and time to be yourself? If yes, that's fantastic. But if even one of the answers is no, speak up. You should be able to stand up for yourself.

Nevertheless, this may be easier said than done. Saying no or challenging someone's behavior can be tough, especially if you aren't used to it. However, as you practice setting and maintaining healthy boundaries, most likely, you'll grow more comfortable expressing your feelings and desires. Over time, you'll be able to find that being true to yourself and your own needs leads to greater self-respect, healthier relationships, and more fulfilling life. So embrace the process and trust that you're moving toward a positive change.

CAN BOUNDARIES WORK FOR NARCISSISTS

It's probable that your difficulty in establishing healthy boundaries is not entirely your fault. Your upbringing can have a huge impact on this ability. Perhaps you grew up feeling that your thoughts and feelings were unimportant. Maybe you had a domineering parent or sibling and found it easier to give in to them rather than stand your ground. Or maybe you subconsciously emulate the behavior of one of your accommodating parents. Although the patterns of behavior you learnt in childhood become strongly ingrained, you probably might not even consciously realize their impact or ever think about your upbringing in this context.

Whatever the reason, it is possible that this behavior continued into adulthood. So when you met your ex, they might have noticed that you didn't have a clear sense of self. You could have been someone who was unsure about your own wants and needs, which may have made it easier for them to influence you. In short, you might have been the type of person they felt comfortable exhibiting their narcissistic behaviors around.

During your time together, your ex might have taken advantage of you. They could have treated you however they wanted, frequently getting their way. They may have influenced how you spent your time and money. And whenever you tried to stand up for yourself, they may have reacted with anger, shouting you down, or gaslighting you to make you feel that you were the one in the wrong. As a result, you may have continued to believe that your needs and wants were not as important or adapted them to accommodate your ex. They might still be treating you poorly and doing whatever they want, as for this to continuously happen, your boundaries would have still been too loose.

But if narcissists don't have any respect or consideration for other people, why would they respect your boundaries? Even if you had healthy, firm boundaries in place, wouldn't they just ignore them? Well, they will more than likely try to. If they are used to getting their own way, they will undoubtedly try to continue to manipulate you. In fact, if you introduce boundaries now, they are likely to become very annoyed and double down on their efforts. In the short term, you may need to brace yourself for their anger, attempts to use the children against you, blame-shifting, pushing back against agreements in your plan, and generally, being more volatile and uncooperative.

In this light, let's revisit the house analogy. Your ex is used to letting themselves into your property whenever they feel like it. They come in at all hours, take what they want, move things around, break things, make a mess, and then leave you to pick up all the pieces. Now, you've had enough and decided to put a new lock on the door. So what do they do? They try to find another way in, through the window, basement, or chimney. You block all of those entry points as well. Now they're getting angry. They're hammering on the door at all hours, hurling abuse at you through the letterbox, and trying to find ways to entice you to open the door. But if you stay firm, stand your ground, and maintain all the locks, eventually, the narcissist will grow bored and frustrated and will most likely seek out another house with no locks on the doors.

The firmer your boundaries are and the more consistently you stick to them, the sooner your ex will understand that they can no longer push you around. Determine what you will and won't tolerate, be firm but fair, and maintain consistency.

HEALTHY BOUNDARIES TO SET WHEN CO-PARENTING

Of course, no one can tell you what your personal boundaries should be. That is entirely up to you; it isn't one size fits all. However, there are a few boundaries recommended to set when it comes to co-parenting.

Keeping the children out of it

Probably the most important boundary you can set in co-parenting is shielding the children from inappropriate behavior. Make it clear to your ex that you are not prepared to have the children dragged into arguments or used to communicate with you. How your ex treats the children while they are at their house is not something you can control. However, you can tell your ex that you are not prepared to have them neglect the children or have them use the children against you in any way.

Keeping your personal life separate

It is only courteous to inform your ex of major changes to your life that will affect the children, such as house moves and new partners. However, they do not need to know anything else about your personal life, and this should be a firm boundary for you. Any attempts to pry, question, persuade, or strong-arm information out of you should be met with firm denial. This also goes for trying to obtain personal information through other means, such as snooping on social media or asking your friends.

Communication boundaries

You should have a clear idea about what you are willing to accept in terms of communication. Is text-messaging you ok, or should your ex exclusively be using email or an agreed app? What times of the day are acceptable for them to contact you and/or the children? Are they keeping you satisfactorily informed about what is going on with the children? Are they being respectful in the language they use? If they are not meeting the boundaries that you set in this area, you need to let them know.

Respecting the parenting plan

A parenting plan is an agreement between separated parents outlining the details regarding their children's care and the division of related responsibilities. This may include agreements such as custody arrangements, visitation schedules, financial responsibilities, and dispute resolution strategies. This is definitely a boundary that you should stick to firmly. If they are neglecting their agreed-upon duties, not showing up when they are supposed to, or not paying you what they should, they are overstepping your boundaries. You need to make it very clear to them that this is behavior that you will not tolerate. If you have not established a parenting plan yet, don't worry, the next chapter will go over it.

Respecting your time with the children

Some narcissists will try to encroach upon your time with the children. They will drop by unannounced, call the children at all hours, or will bring them back late, eating into your time. This should be a firm boundary. Since you do not interrupt and step in on their time with the children, they should respect your time in return.

Treating you with respect

You are no longer in a relationship with your ex. You left because of the way they treated you: belittling you, manipulating you, demanding you behave in a particular way, etc. You no longer have to accept that behavior. You can finally act with respect for yourself and make it clear that treating you with disrespect will no longer be accepted.

HOW TO SET BOUNDARIES THE RIGHT WAY

So you know why setting boundaries is so important and some of the boundaries you should consider. But how do you go about setting boundaries, and how can you enforce them so that your narcissistic ex will listen?

Decide on your boundaries

What are you willing to put up with? What won't you tolerate? Have some time to yourself to reflect on what is important to you. What behaviors do you wish your co-parent would display? How about honesty? Respect? Fairness? What would your ideal co-parent look like?

Now look at where their behavior really infuriates you. Do you find yourself longing for them to just be on time for once? Do you wish they would stop criticizing everything you do? Consider how their actions make you feel. Simultaneously, consider the physical manifestations of these feelings. Anything that is causing a physical reaction, such as clenched muscles or a raised heart rate, is something you clearly feel strongly about.

Think very carefully here. It's possible that you might think you're willing to tolerate a certain behavior simply because you've grown used to it over time. This familiarity could cause the behavior to wash over you, leaving you desensitized to its effects. Consider to what extent you got used to it and to what extent it is something you don’t want to tolerate. You must decide whether you are ok continuing to let that behavior wash over you or whether you are going to put your foot down from now on. Keep in mind that longstanding patterns might be less obvious to you, so it's essential to take the time to think about your feelings carefully.

Finally, think about other people and what they expect and demand from you. Are there others in your life that you feel take advantage of you or don’t listen to you? This could also give you a clue about where you need firmer boundaries.

Start small

If you’ve never been scuba-diving before, you wouldn’t just jump in and hope for the best; it’s a good idea to learn how to swim first. If you’ve spent your whole life with very loose boundaries, it will feel quite strange and a bit scary to start telling people no or that you're not happy with something. So pick something small to begin with and work your way up. As you find your voice and build up your confidence, it will seem easier and easier to express your own needs in a calm, kind way.

You know your ex is going to be difficult, so you could start by dipping your toes into the world of boundaries with friends and family first. It may be hard in the beginning, and they might not understand what you are trying to achieve. Moreover, you might worry that you are disappointing them or letting them down, but ultimately, if they really have your back, they won't be angry or disappointed in you, even if it might take them time to get used to the changes you are implementing. True allies will respect your boundaries and your decisions and should be happy that you are sticking up for yourself.

Be clear and firm

Don't leave your ex in any doubt of your decisions and intentions. If you can't take your son to football practice, don't tell them you probably can't. You may think that means no, but your ex will most likely think it is unconfirmed. If they are rude to you, don't just ignore them. You may think that they will get the message that you're annoyed, but they won't know or care and will simply do it again. Whatever boundary you are enforcing, you need to be clear. This doesn't mean that you have to be rude. Just be firm but fair. For instance, you could try using statements similar to those listed below:

"I'm really sorry. I won't be able to take x to football practice for you on Saturday."

"I'd really appreciate it if you could ask me before you xxx."

"Please respect my privacy. I need you to stop posting information about me on social media."

Offer solutions

Establishing boundaries when communicating with your narcissist ex leads to the next point: try to use a solutions-based approach. Let's say your ex is telling you that they can't pick up the children on Tuesday and asking you to drop them off instead. You could say, "I'm sorry, I can't drop them off." You are well within your rights to stick to your boundaries and say no, but they're probably going to get angry and blame you for not helping them. Instead, try to offer an alternative or steer them towards the solution rather than the problem. Here, you might say, "I'm afraid I won't be able to drop them at yours. Could you pick them up earlier or later, perhaps?"

Using a solution-based approach works for most situations. You don't have to solve everyone's problems for them, but it can help to guide them towards helping themselves. It also softens the blow so that you don't seem quite so blunt. Have a look below at the solution-based statements that you could apply to your life:

"I'm afraid I can't make it on Saturday, but it would be great if we could catch up next week."

"I'd really appreciate it if you could ask me before you xxx. If I'm not around, you can just drop me a text."

"I just don't have the capacity to help you at the moment. I can help next week if that works?"

Don't elaborate

Even if you are offering an alternative or a solution, remember that you do not have to offer an explanation. You do not have to explain your boundaries or justify them. You may wish to tell your friend why you can't make it to their party, but you definitely don't need to elaborate on your boundaries to your ex. This could just draw them into a discussion in which they have the opportunity to twist your words and manipulate you. Ask them to stop a specific behavior and leave it at that.

Define consequences

It is all very well having boundaries, but what will happen if people overstep or ignore them? If you don't impose any consequences, your ex won't care and will continue to disrespect them. Instead of "Please, do not continue to speak to me that way," you could say, "If you continue to speak to me that way, I will hang up the phone." Instead of "I will not accept you dropping the children off two hours late," you could say, "If you cannot bring the children back on time, I will deduct the time from your days with them."

Don't feel guilty

This might be a hard one to get to grips with. If you are used to putting everyone else's needs before your own, it might be difficult for you to stand up for your own needs without feeling guilty. Don't. Your time, your needs, and your wants are just as important as everyone else's. Tell yourself and others that you have the right to time off. You deserve to be treated with respect. Stop apologizing for that and start treating yourself as you would treat others.

Expect pushback

Prepare yourself for some resistance from your ex. They're not going to be happy when you start enforcing your boundaries. They may quietly sulk and find subtle ways of getting at you. Or they may be like that toddler in the supermarket after you tell them they can't have any candy. Either way, they're probably not just going to smile and say, "Fair enough." But if you know what is coming, you can prepare for it.

Hold firm

Finally, whatever happens, stick to your boundaries. If you have decided you will not tolerate your ex dropping the children off late, don't let it go one day but not the next. Just like establishing discipline with children, you must be consistent. If you only uphold your boundaries some of the time, there will be enough room for your ex to manipulate you and to get their own way.

SUMMARY

Enforcing physical boundaries is generally easier, as you don't tolerate strangers wandering through your home or damaging your possessions. However, defending your personal boundaries can be more challenging. But it's essential to establish healthy personal boundaries to ensure your needs and wants are respected and to prevent yourself from becoming burnt out, manipulated, or hurt. To achieve that, simply be clear and firm about what you expect and present consequences for what happens if the boundaries are not respected. Hold firm, no matter what happens, and do not explain your reasons or be drawn into a discussion. Finally, do not feel guilty for setting boundaries. Remember that your needs are just as important as anyone else's.

Narcissists are very good at finding people with unhealthy boundaries and exploiting them to their advantage. If you don't stand up for yourself or believe that your needs are worth respecting, narcissists will likely treat you however they please. On the other hand, if you can learn to assert yourself and enforce your personal boundaries in a healthy way, narcissists will most probably get the message and will be forced to acknowledge and respect them.

Take the time to decide what behaviors you are willing to put up with and what you will not stand for. As a minimum, you have a right to expect that your ex follows the parenting plan and that they communicate with you respectfully and using the agreed method. You should demand that they keep the children out of any conflict and that they do not encroach upon your time with them. You should expect them to stay out of your personal life.

Action items

- Take some time to consider your current personal boundaries and identify areas where they may be weak or unhealthy. Reflect on how these boundaries have affected your relationships, especially with narcissistic individuals.
- Make a list of behaviors and situations that you are not willing to tolerate. These nonnegotiable will serve as the foundation for your healthy boundaries.
- Clearly communicate your boundaries to others, especially your ex-partner, at the next opportunity. Be

firm and assertive in your communication, but also remain respectful and open to compromise when appropriate. Share the nonnegotiables you determined from the previous step.

CHAPTER 7

PARALLEL PARENTING AND PARENTING PLANS

Handling the difficulties of co-parenting with a narcissistic ex can seem impossible. As you've seen in Chapter One, the traditional approach to cooperative parenting might not be achievable in such situations. So what is the alternative? Parallel parenting, which you will explore in this chapter.

Parallel parenting is a strategy designed to minimize conflict and ensure a more harmonious parenting experience when dealing with a difficult ex. This slightly different approach might be the key to maintaining a healthier environment for you and your children. In this chapter, you'll delve into what parallel parenting involves, how it compares to co-parenting, and how it might work for you, creating a less stressful and more manageable parenting experience.

CO-PARENTING AND PARALLEL PARENTING

Think of almost any team sport. Soccer, basketball, synchronized swimming. Any of these sports involves more than one person working on scoring goals/hoops/points together. Naturally, everyone on the team must follow the same rules, and everyone on the team needs to appreciate that it isn't all about them.

This analogy illustrates what co-parenting, or cooperative parenting, is. Both parties take on equal responsibilities, working together for the common goal of raising the children well. They agree on the rules and understand that it's about the children, not themselves. The two parents may not get along, but they can communicate openly and civilly. They can meet in person or talk on the phone without arguments, and they can attend events such as school consultations and sporting events together.

On the other hand, parallel parenting is where parents work towards the same goal, but they go about it in their own way. Picture it like fishing. Each angler is on the lake for essentially the same reason, but they have their own methods, their own bait and tackle, and their own schedules. They are not in opposition, but they are also not working together, and the communication (if any) is minimal.

With parallel parenting, each parent decides on their own rules and their own approach to parenting. They don't attend parent-teacher conferences or performances together, and they communicate in a structured way through email, texts, or specialized apps.

WHICH APPROACH TO TAKE

Co-parenting: pros and cons

Co-parenting offers several advantages, such as sharing parenting responsibilities, providing consistency for children in terms of discipline and expectations, and helping children feel more secure seeing their parents get along. It is generally easier when there are two people pulling in the same direction. If you can be civil, attend meetings together, and pick up the slack if the other parent is sick or busy, it does take away some of the stress. You may not be completely conflict-free, but if there is someone else whom you can rely on, it does make things easier than having to do everything yourself.

Co-parenting may also be better for children in most circumstances. If they know their parents can get along on some level and aren't going to tear each other to pieces in the interval of the school play, it will be far less stressful for them. If you are able to agree on a shared parenting approach in terms of discipline and expectations, the children will know that what is expected of them is more or less the same in both houses, giving them much more consistency.

On the face of it, there seem to be very few disadvantages to co-parenting. However, that really depends on the relationship you have with your ex. If everyone *is* working together for the good of the children and has no ulterior motives, then great. But if your ex exhibits a high amount of narcissistic behaviors and tendencies, co-parenting gives them an awful lot of ground for manipulating you and getting their own way. You may be civil with each other at the moment, but co-parenting does leave you more room for conflict than parallel parenting, as it requires constant communication and negotiation between parents.

Parallel parenting: pros and cons

Parallel parenting allows each parent to establish their own rules and parenting style, reducing conflict by limiting communication. You set the rules in your own house. You make your own decisions. You do not continually have to bounce things off your ex, and there's no justifying your choices. This allows you to parent in a much more fluid way, as you do not have to wait for responses and feedback.

Parallel parenting requires less contact than co-parenting. What contact is necessary is done in a structured way and is usually written. This means that you will have far less communication with your ex, which should result in far less conflict. Not only will this be much better for your own mental health, but it will also be beneficial for your children, as they are not continually caught in the crossfire. That's why this approach is great in high-conflict situations—it shields children from ongoing disputes. However, parallel parenting also means functioning alone and requires letting go of control over what happens in the other parent's household.

If your ex no longer has any input into how you manage the children when they are at your house, you also must let go of what happens at theirs. If your ex can't call the children at yours whenever they feel like it, you also have to abide by the same rules.

Choosing the best approach

As you can see, both styles of separated parenting have their pros and cons. You cannot definitively say that co-parenting is superior to parallel parenting or vice versa, just as you cannot say that basketball is superior to fishing. The best choice depends on the specific situation and the personalities involved. There are no strict rules when it comes to choosing a parenting style. You might start with parallel parenting and transition to co-parenting as the situation improves, or you may need to adapt and change your approach as needed. It's possible to include elements from both styles to create a customized strategy that best suits your circumstances.

For instance, with an ex who is more of a "closet" narcissist, you might well be able to attend school meetings together. Narcissists often have a public persona which is perfectly charming. In this case, they are unlikely to show their true colors in public. But you might want to lean more towards parallel parenting for the rest of the time if they are likely to try and manipulate you behind closed doors.

Perhaps you have an ex who continually tries to prove they are the best parent. Co-parenting might be a good option here because, at least, they are focusing on the children. They might be more flexible with the schedule if they are busy trying to show you how much more dedicated they are. However, it could be that you need to let them handle their own household without any input from you. After all, they think they know best and probably won't appreciate any of your suggestions or concerns.

For highly narcissistic, volatile, and manipulative ex-partners, parallel parenting is the recommended approach, as it minimizes conflict and helps maintain a more peaceful environment for the children.

It is usually evident which approach is best for you, and you will probably lean more toward one style than the other. You *can* change things up if they aren't working or if they are going better than expected. However, where narcissists are concerned, consistency is often better than fluidity.

WHAT TO COVER IN A PARENTING PLAN

Whether co-parenting or parallel parenting, you need a detailed parenting plan. It can help to have it endorsed by a court as part of your custody arrangements. To help you get started, you will find a parenting plan template and other valuable resources that you can easily access by scanning the QR code or following the link at the end of the book.

When creating a parenting plan, here are some areas you will need to consider time and accessibility, decision-making, finances, communication and conflict resolution, and changes and updates, which are all discussed in the following sections.

TIME AND ACCESSIBILITY

Schedule and custody arrangements

A parenting plan should include answers to the following time-related questions: where will the children be staying, and on which days? Who will be picking up/dropping off the children at each handover, and where will this take place? Make the arrangements as detailed as possible. Don't just say that your ex will have the children on a Tuesday, and you'll have them on a Wednesday. Make it very clear who is responsible for dropping them off at school and who will be picking them up. If they are going directly from one house to another, state what time. Be specific with transportation, locations, times, and any related expenses.

If you are parallel parenting, you should maintain minimal face-to-face contact. Pick up and drop off the children at a neutral place rather than at each other's homes. Ideally, find a location where the children can be left for a few minutes until you can collect them, such as a grandparent's house.

Holidays, vacations, and special occasions

Ensure you include holiday and vacation arrangements in your parenting plan. For instance, how will the school holidays be covered? What about special occasions such as Christmas and birthdays? How much notice is required? Do you need to inform each other about where you are going? How will this information be shared?

Alterations to the schedule

Life happens, and sometimes the agreed schedule needs to be adjusted. Thus, contingencies in such cases should be reflected in your parenting plan. Consider and add to the plan how you handle these instances. What is the process if one of you needs to swap or cancel a day? How much notice should be given? On the other hand, you may wish to implement a strict no alterations policy to maintain structure and minimize conflict.

This includes the concept of the right of first refusal. If one parent is unable to care for the children during their assigned time, the other parent should have the opportunity to step in before any alternative arrangements (like babysitters or family members) are considered. Identify what access grandparents/aunts/uncles have regarding looking after the children.

PARENTING AND DECISION-MAKING

Specify how decisions concerning the children's education, healthcare, religion, and extracurricular activities will be made. This can be joint decision-making or one parent having the final say. Other major decisions can include things like travel, driving, or vehicle use.

Schools and education

Deciding on the school your children will attend can be complex, especially if you reside in different towns. How will the school communicate with you? Who will be present at parent-teacher meetings?

Remember that if you are parallel parenting, you will need to ensure that the school is aware of the situation and that they communicate with both parents equally.

Health and medicines

Consider how you deal will with any ongoing medical issues. Who is responsible for doctor, hospital, or dentist visits? How will you keep each other informed?

In parallel parenting, despite minimal communication, this is one area where it is important to keep each other up to date with all health matters. Find a neutral way to discuss these issues, such as via email or a third-party app.

Discipline and parenting guidelines

Agree on certain rules to be uniformly enforced at both homes. What happens when you need to apply a punishment? Does the other parent need to be informed? Include bedtime and screen time rules.

With parallel parenting, remember that you decide on all the discipline and expectations in your home, and you do not need to discuss or share this with your ex.

FINANCES

How will you divide the children's expenses? What will be classed as a joint expense? How will you transfer funds, and when? This can cover alimony/child support payments and how to handle unforeseen costs.

Make it very clear how finances will be split. Draw up a comprehensive list of what is considered a joint expense. While it may seem straightforward, there is a gray area here, leaving room for potential manipulation from your ex if it's not specifically outlined in the plan. Some things to consider are:

- Birthday/Christmas presents.
- Gifts for friends' birthday parties.
- Clothing and footwear.
- Haircuts.
- School trips.
- Dinner money.
- Children's allowances.
- Extracurricular activities.
- After-school/breakfast clubs.
- Travel expenses.

By defining these expenses upfront, you will ensure a fair and transparent financial arrangement.

COMMUNICATION AND CONFLICT RESOLUTION

Defining expectations around communicating and resolving conflicts will help you maintain a more stable co-parenting arrangement. Specifying boundaries will create a more predictable and consistent environment for both you and your children, while a defined conflict resolution strategy will help you both handle disagreements objectively and reduce unnecessary escalation.

Communication and boundaries

When it comes to communication and setting boundaries, you need to decide how you will keep each other informed about your children. When are phone calls appropriate? How will you communicate with the children when they are away, and how often? You may wish to use a co-parenting app, such as the ones recommended in the resources link at the end of this book. These have built-in functions specifically for divided families and can keep everything fully documented and in one place. Set expectations for response times and respectful communication.

If you are parallel parenting, remember that you should keep communication to a minimum. Your ex should not be calling or messaging you unexpectedly, and all communication should revolve solely around the children.

Conflict resolution

If not already outlined in the communication section, outline a specific method where disagreements will be addressed. This should always be using a method that leaves a record of the conversation. If you can't agree, decide if one parent gets the final say in the decision-making areas discussed earlier. For instance, one parent might make the final decision regarding education, while the other may make the final decision about healthcare. If the conflict remains unresolved between the two of you, ensure you have an escalation process. This could include professional mediation, appointing a neutral third party to make a final decision, or, as a last resort, taking the matter to court. More information is given on this in the next chapter. You could also agree on a cooling-off period—a mutually agreed break if discussions become too heated. This allows both parents to calm down and reflect before resuming the conversation.

CHANGES AND UPDATES

New partners and significant changes

Life moves forward, and new relationships and other changes are bound to occur. So how do you address this in your new parenting plan? When can new partners be introduced to the children? How will you keep each other informed? One approach is to hold off introducing new partners until the relationship is serious and well established. Define what steps should be taken if one parent plans to live together with a new partner. This can include discussing with the other parent and children to prepare them for the change. It is important to note that while new partners can be supportive figures, they are not replacing the other parent. Parents should agree to be respectful of new partners.

Life changes like job loss, changes in financial stability, health issues, or moving to a new location can impact the terms of the parenting plan.

In the world of parallel parenting, it's essential to maintain boundaries around personal information. You can share necessary updates, such as a change in residence, but no more than what's required to follow the parenting plan.

Updates and modifications

Establish a procedure for reviewing and updating the parenting plan as needed to accommodate changing circumstances or the evolving needs of the children. It is recommended to review the plan yearly or perhaps at a different frequency that suits both parents better.

You will also need a method to suggest unscheduled changes, including guidelines for advanced notice. But remember that flexibility is key. As your children grow and you experience changes, the plan should adapt accordingly.

As you can see, there is an awful lot to think about. And your situation is even more challenging because you're doing this with someone who might not always play fair during a period of heightened emotion and stress. It's not going to be a walk in the park, but remember, your primary goal is always the well-being and happiness of your children.

HOW TO MAKE A PARENTING PLAN WITH A NARCISSIST

By this point, you may have a clearer understanding of your desired parenting plan and how you want it to function. Maybe you are leaning towards more of a co-parenting approach, or perhaps you think parallel parenting will better suit your situation. Let's have a look now at how to formulate your plan effectively.

1. Think about what your ideal situation would be. Let's face it—your ex probably won't agree to everything you want, but having a goal will help you stay focused when they try to confuse or pressure you.
2. Next, you need to discuss the plan with your ex. If you think a face-to-face meeting is possible, arrange one. Make the location somewhere completely neutral and of no significance to your history. Somewhere public is best, such as a café or a library. It may also be a good idea to bring a third party, like a lawyer or mediator, to keep things calm. As you know, narcissists generally act differently in public and are more likely to be civil and agreeable if there is someone else in the room.
3. If an in-person meeting is out of the question, a written discussion can be an alternative. This might take longer but has benefits in that everything is recorded and can be referred to in the future.
4. Talk about each point in the plan one at a time. Remember that you are no longer together, and you do not have to agree with everything your ex says. If you can't agree on something, stay calm. If you start to feel angry or upset, suggest postponing that part of the discussion to a later time.
5. Take breaks and give yourselves room to have a rest and to reflect on things individually. The entire process doesn't need to be completed in one sitting.
6. When you think you have reached an agreement about something, write it down. You don't want your ex coming back a day later, claiming that's not what they agreed to. If you are discussing things in writing, be sure to make it very clear what has been finalized and what is still under discussion.

7. Make the plan as detailed as possible. It isn't petty to include small details; it will save you a lot of headaches in the future if you can be as specific as possible. Don't give them any wiggle room. The more specific you are, the less they can use any gray areas to their own advantage.
8. When it's all written up, you should both sign it. Consider drawing up the final version with the help of an attorney to make it legally binding.

SUMMARY

Co-parenting and parallel parenting are slightly different approaches, but ultimately share the same goal—to put your children first and ensure they receive what they need from both parents. Co-parenting offers a bit more flexibility and encourages regular, open communication. You should be able to discuss issues regarding the children freely, attend meetings together, and maintain a civil and respectful collaboration.

However, depending on your ex's level of narcissism, co-parenting might be a challenge. In such cases, parallel parenting may be a strategy to keep the children as the main focus while minimizing communication with your ex. You can essentially parent the way that you want to without interference, provided that you are prepared to face the fact that your ex has the same freedom.

Finally, whether you discuss these arrangements in person or via email, you need to ensure that everything is documented. The final written version of the plan should be signed by both of you and, ideally, be legally binding to ensure everyone's commitment.

Action items

- Reflect on the two primary methods of parenting post-separation: co-parenting and parallel parenting. Consider the dynamics with your ex, the characteristics of your relationship, and the needs of your children. Which method aligns better with your situation?
- If you have not already, begin to draft a parenting plan, considering all aspects mentioned, such as time and accessibility, holidays, special occasions, decision-making, finances, and communication. You can scan the QR code provided at the end of the book, or follow the given link, to access a parenting plan template and other helpful resources.
- If you have a parenting plan already, ensure all required elements are covered. Whichever approach you take, you will need to make sure that your parenting plan is as watertight as possible. Avoid leaving loopholes that will allow them to manipulate the situation to their advantage. Make a list of absolutely every detail that needs to be covered in the plan. Think about the day-to-day schedule, holidays, and how you will deal with any necessary alterations. Iron out exactly how your finances will be managed. Look at agreed methods of communication. Consider any particular arrangements your children need, such as medicines, schooling, and discipline. Leave no stone unturned.
- Develop a conflict resolution strategy and identify a method for escalating unresolved disagreements if required. Ensure a schedule is set to regularly review and update your parenting plan as your children grow and circumstances change.

CHAPTER 8

MANAGING HIGH-CONFLICT CO-PARENTING

So, you've been following all the advice in this book. You've been calm and measured in all your interactions. You've limited contact and communicate mostly in writing. You've been the reasonable, empathetic parent that your children need, and you've set and stuck to your boundaries. But things still may not be working. If that's the case, you still have options. So let's have a look at what you can do when your ex won't play ball and what you can do if they really turn nasty.

WHEN THEY IGNORE, PUSH, OR TEST YOUR BOUNDARIES

You've set your boundaries, but your ex is just willfully ignoring them. There's no respect for what you have said or asked for, and they continue to do what they want and treat you badly. Where do you go from here?

You might not want to hear it, but the first piece of advice is to take a good hard look at yourself. If you are not used to setting boundaries, it is easy to feel guilty about them. Maybe you default to wanting to help others. Maybe you feel your needs are not as important as others'. Maybe you hate conflict and will give in just to avoid it. But remember, having boundaries is not about being selfish. It isn't about just getting what you want and to hell with everyone else. It is about recognizing your own needs and giving those needs a voice. It isn't self-indulgent to want uninterrupted time with your children. It isn't selfish to want others to speak to you with respect. Recognize the importance of your needs and stop feeling guilty.

Are your boundaries clear enough? If you aren't being absolutely transparent about what you will and won't put up with, you can't expect others to understand and respect those boundaries. Don't give your ex any excuse for not abiding by your rules; if they can wriggle out of it, claiming they didn't understand, they will. For this reason, you need to make those boundaries watertight so there is absolutely no space for misunderstanding.

Are you being firm when implementing those boundaries? Every time your ex is crossing them, are you communicating to them this is an issue? Because if you let it go, just once, they won't take your boundaries seriously. Any of them. Don't be afraid to say no or to tell your ex that their behavior is unacceptable. Yes, they might get angry, but remember—short-term pain for long-term gain.

If your boundaries are definitely clear and consistent, but your ex is still pushing back or ignoring you, what then? There are strategies you can use that will help you when dealing with a narcissistic ex who disrespects your boundaries.

Hold firm. Do not be bullied into giving in. It may take many reiterations of the boundary before they finally get the message that you're serious about it.

Follow through on consequences. If you say you are going to hang up the phone if they carry on shouting at you, do so. If you say you will not allow the children to answer unscheduled phone calls from them, don't. It's no good threatening to do or not do something if you aren't prepared to see it through. Let them know your boundaries are serious by offering consequences and sticking to them.

Stay calm. Remember not to be lured into any arguments. This will only give your ex an opening to gain the upper hand. Stay measured in your responses; channel that grey rock. Don't explain or expand upon your decisions—just state them clearly and move on.

Document everything. Keep all your written communications and messages. Make notes on their behavior. If you can, record conversations. This will not only give you evidence if your word is challenged in the future, but it will also give you a greater understanding of patterns in their behavior and a chance to identify any weak spots in yours.

Finally, remember that it gets easier with practice. The more you reiterate your boundaries and follow through on consequences, the more it will become second nature. Over time, your ex will hopefully get the message that you are not a pushover and that they cannot manipulate you into getting what they want. Then, they may attempt to get the narcissistic supply from easier sources where they don't have to work quite so hard.

RECOGNIZING SIGNS OF ABUSE: A QUICK REFRESHER FROM CHAPTER FOUR

Although Chapter Four has touched on this subject, it bears repeating. Any form of abuse—be it physical, emotional, or psychological—directed towards you or your child is a severe red flag. This includes actions that demean, intimidate, manipulate, or harm your child physically or emotionally. Remember to keep a watchful eye for any signs of distress or changes in your child's behavior and take appropriate action.

When they're using your child to control you

It's one thing having your ex disrespect or belittle you. It's another matter when they start using the children to try to control your behavior. In this case, they might:

- Try and stop the children from contacting you or spending time with you.
- Fail to collect them or drop them off according to the schedule.
- Try to monopolize the children's time when they are with you.
- Refuse to care for the children when they know you have important plans.
- Refuse to enforce basic routines or discipline to make it harder for you to manage the children at your house.
- Buy costly gifts or take the children on expensive trips to try to win their favor.
- Make threats to gain sole custody.

Some of these behaviors may not even be in their own interest, but they'll do these things just to try and regain their power over you and to show you who's in control. That's the sort of person you're dealing with here. And how do you deal with someone who is that spiteful?

As we've said before, stay calm. Nothing good will come of you getting riled up and arguing about it. The worst thing you can do in this situation is to react with fire; all it will do is signal to them that their behavior is getting the desired results. As you know, they will likely use an argument to make you out to be the bad guy. So don't go there, however hard it may be.

If you haven't already, consider parallel parenting. Limit all contact with your ex and communicate through emails, text, or a co-parenting app wherever possible. This will give them fewer opportunities to conveniently "forget" that they were picking the children up this time. It will also ensure that you have everything in writing, so if they consistently flout the agreements in your parenting plan, you have the fuel to take the matter up with a mediator or your attorney.

Do not rely on your ex for any additional childcare above and beyond what is agreed in the schedule. If you have important meetings or events to attend when you are due to have the children, find an alternative. Ask your parents or a friend or find a babysitter. If they are constantly turning up with the children claiming they can't look after them, you'll have some backup options in place. And again, if you document everything, you'll have grounds to take the matter further.

Parallel parenting also enables you to keep your houses completely separate and focus on your own behaviors and your own parenting. So your ex might buy the children a load of expensive stuff. So they might take them on fancy trips. It doesn't matter. Lots of people may be in this situation, and many of them may observe the same thing—that the children don't really care. They will easily adjust to having less at your house as long as they have a good time with you and you give them your love, understanding, and attention. At the end of the day, these things matter more, especially if love and attention are lacking at your ex's house.

Will your children really struggle to abide by your rules and routines if your ex is less than consistent with discipline at theirs? Will your children prefer to be at the "fun house" where they can stay up late and eat what they want? Maybe in the short term. But honestly, children like routines and boundaries. Without them, they tend to feel confused and unsettled. So stick with what you are doing. Draw up a family agreement so that everyone knows the rules. Most children will switch pretty easily between houses as long as they know what is expected.

Basically, be the better parent. Stick to your end of the parenting arrangements to the letter. Stay calm and rise above any of their schemes to try and gain the upper hand. Concentrate on your own house and on enjoying your time with the children when they are with you.

When they're trying to alienate your child

Possibly the worst weapon in the narcissist's arsenal is parental alienation. This is when they will try to turn their children against you, their other parent, in a calculated campaign to paint them as the bad guy. They may speak ill of you to your child, blame you for the separation, or attempt to obstruct your time together. It can result in a complete breakdown of your relationship with the children and can have devastating long-term effects for both you and your children. Recognizing these attempts early can help you address the issue and take the necessary steps.

The narcissist may blame you for their feelings of loss concerning your relationship and may hate the fact that they are no longer in control. Remember that locked box of vulnerability that they keep buried? Well, it may appear as if you forced it open, and, just like Pandora, unleashed hell. Due to their narcissistic mindset, they often may not be able to separate their own feelings and their need to hate you from those of their children. In *extreme* cases, the narcissist could end up consciously or subconsciously shifting these feelings onto the children, effectively trying to force them to hate you as much as they do.

They could barrage the children with continual negative comments, encourage disrespect, try to isolate them, muscle in on your time, manipulate the children into unquestioning loyalty towards themselves, and paint you out to be dangerous, untrustworthy, or disinterested. The child could join in with vilifying you—a behavior that is reinforced with reward and punishment. Eventually, this may result in the child no longer wanting any relationship with you at all.

Warning signs

If you are worried that this is happening or might happen to you, here are some of the early warning signs to look out for:

- Your child is trying to exclude you; for example, by asking you not to attend school meetings or always requesting their other parent take them to after-school activities.
- Your child no longer wants to stay overnight.

- Your child has become very argumentative.
- Your child doesn't seem to want your affection anymore; for example, they reject cuddles and do not offer any in return.
- Your child becomes very withdrawn and will not engage with you.
- Your child starts calling you by your name rather than "Mom" or "Dad."
- Your child persistently criticizes you but offers no valid explanations.
- Your child also rejects or criticizes your family and friends.
- Your ex persistently prevents you from seeing or speaking to your child.
- Your ex continually disrespects your time with your child; for example, by turning up unannounced or planning exciting trips on your weekend with the child, thus making the child choose.
- Your ex stops sharing information about your child, including school reports, likes and dislikes, etc.

Of course, you need to be aware that some of these behaviors might be normal. Your child has been experiencing a parental breakup, which might cause temporary withdrawal or feelings of resentment. Also, children can be fickle; they can choose a favorite parent; they can be stubborn, and as they grow older, they frequently exercise their free will. Teenagers, particularly, will often go through a phase of hating Mom or Dad. This may be a perfectly standard behavior and not necessarily a cause for alarm.

You know your children. You'll be the best judge of whether their behavior is typical or not. Remember the importance of communication from Chapter Five? Here's another reason to establish great communication with your child as early as possible: If you have a relationship built on openness and honesty, you will know immediately if their actions are part of the normal ebb and flow of childhood or if you have a more serious problem on your hands.

Prevention

Try not to worry. Parental alienation sounds like a terrifying situation to be in, but it isn't a given. Prevention, as they say, is better than cure. If your children are small and/or the breakup is new, revisit the advice in this book about establishing a great relationship with your children. The more you can present yourself as someone they can love and trust and the better your communication with your children, the better your chances are that they will continue to love you through thick and thin. Reiterate how much you love them and be interested in what they have to say. Do all you can to contradict anything your ex might tell your children about how disinterested you are or how little you care about them.

Firm up that parenting agreement and stick to those boundaries. Don't give your ex any leeway when it comes to muscling in on your time with the children. Do not allow them to call at all hours or pop around whenever they feel like it.

Once again, write everything down. Use a co-parenting app or a text-messaging service that allows you to save all your messages or communicate strictly by email. Consider resisting getting your children a phone of their own for as long as possible—this way, all their messages must go through you and can also be recorded. Eventually, of course, your ex will be able to contact your child independently, but until then, you can monitor what is going on. In addition to recording your messages, keep notes. Record your children's comments and behavior, especially if anything seems off or uncharacteristic.

If you suspect alienation

If you are seeing signs of strange behavior, and you think your ex might be attempting to alienate your children, stay calm. It is easier said than done, but don't do anything in anger. Take some deep breaths and slow down. You're first reaction will probably be to have it out with your ex. But it's a bad idea—they will only deny everything, and you will let them know that they are getting to you. You might also be tempted to challenge your children on their attitudes and opinions. This could also backfire, as you will be putting them in the middle of a difficult situation. Making them uncomfortable or wary of saying anything will only fuel their distrust.

Instead, back off. Create an environment for your child in which they are not pressured or judged. Give them space and time to release any negative emotions and to talk freely if they wish. If you try to counter their arguments or continually tell them what they are hearing isn't true, they might just feel increased pressure, for which they will resent you. "Remember in order for alienation to be effective, there is a constant barrage of misinformation, manipulation, and pressure. Creating a no-pressure-safe-zone helps your child to decompress" (Hammond, 2019).

Give your child opportunities to run the show. Make time to play with them, but let them decide everything: from what games to play to what you should say and do. Let them be in control. If your children are older, give them opportunities to decide on what activities to do together, what movies to watch, or what food to cook. Giving your child back some control creates a very different environment than the one they will be experiencing at your ex's house. There, they are being told what to say and what to think. So at your house, make their opinions matter and teach them how to make up their own mind.

Last but very definitely not least, speak to an attorney as soon as possible. The sooner you can get some legal advice on the situation, the better. Be patient, continue to record everything, and don't give up.

INCONSISTENT COMMUNICATION AND UNPREDICTABLE BEHAVIOR

One of the primary issues frequently confronted in high-conflict co-parenting scenarios is inconsistent communication and unpredictable behavior, which may lead to a sense of instability and confusion. Examples of this might include sudden changes in established agreements, inconsistent responses to messages or requests, or changes between cooperative and confrontational attitudes.

Counteracting this behavior requires structure and resilience, as discussed earlier. To this end, introduce clear, consistent communication guidelines, focusing on keeping discussions factual and oriented towards the best interests of the children. Avoid letting personal feelings seep into the conversation. Written communication, like emails or texts, can provide a more controlled platform for discussion. Likewise, establishing specific times for communication can also help to instill predictability. Using co-parenting apps can also assist in managing and tracking exchanges. Equally important is managing your own reactions to erratic behavior—avoid responding impulsively, which may escalate the situation. If the unpredictable behavior persists, it might be beneficial to involve a family therapist or mediator to aid in streamlining communication.

MANIPULATING THROUGH GUILT OR COERCION

Manipulation using guilt or coercion is a common but underhanded tactic that can surface in high-conflict parenting situations. This involves using emotional manipulation or guilt-tripping to gain control over situations, create a favorable narrative, or project themselves as the "better" parent.

Detecting this form of manipulation is often tricky as it taps into emotional vulnerabilities. However, signs to look for include attempts to guilt-trip you into changing decisions, distortions of facts to generate sympathy, or unjustly attributing negative outcomes to your actions.

Dealing with such manipulation requires establishing and maintaining strong emotional boundaries. When dealing with guilt or coercion, stay focused on the facts and refrain from getting drawn into emotional arguments. Stand firm in your decisions, especially when they are made with the children's best interests at heart. Seek support from therapists or counselors if needed, as they can provide useful tools and techniques to handle emotional manipulation. If these behaviors continue unabated, engaging a mediator or a family therapist might be a sensible course of action.

EXCESSIVE LITIGATION AND LEGAL HARASSMENT

Another troubling high-conflict behavior is excessive litigation and legal harassment. In these situations, the co-parent uses the legal system as a weapon to inflict distress, exert control, or simply create chaos. This might take the form of frequent threats of legal action or the filing of unnecessary or frivolous lawsuits designed more to harass than to address legitimate issues.

Identifying this behavior requires vigilance. Keep an eye out for any legal threats, both veiled and explicit. Excessive lawsuits or constant referencing of lawyers and legal action can be signs of legal harassment.

The antidote to this behavior is knowledge, preparation, and sometimes, appropriate legal countermeasures. Familiarize yourself with your legal rights and responsibilities. Maintain a thorough record of all interactions, especially those involving threats or actual instances of legal action. Regularly consult with your attorney and rely on their expertise to navigate the sea of legal threats. If the situation escalates, consider pursuing legal remedies, such as filing for a protection order or seeking sanctions for frivolous litigation.

LEGAL CONSIDERATIONS IN HIGH-CONFLICT CO-PARENTING

Navigating the legal landscape of high-conflict co-parenting can often feel like journeying through a labyrinth. But don't let this daunt you. With the right understanding and support, you can master this maze. For this reason, let's delve into the important aspects, from knowing your rights to finding legal counsel and how to handle disputes that may end up in court.

Understanding your legal rights

Grasping your legal rights is paramount in this situation. It's not just beneficial—it's crucial. This knowledge will serve as your roadmap, guiding you as you navigate the twists and turns of your co-parenting journey. Look into details such as custody types, child support regulations, and visitation rights. Remember, laws can vary significantly based on jurisdiction, so it's essential to familiarize yourself with local and federal statutes that apply to you. While there's a wealth of information available online, ensure you're referring to reputable sources to avoid any misinformation.

Seeking legal advice and finding a good attorney

Alright, let's talk about something that can be as intimidating as it is necessary—lawyers. Whether you've been in a courtroom or just watched them on TV, you know how crucial a good attorney can be in the legal process. But let's be real, finding the right attorney feels like trying to find the perfect avocado at the grocery store—it seems simple but can be trickier than you think.

When dealing with high-conflict co-parenting situations, you need more than just legal advice. You need someone who understands your specific situation, can guide you through the legal labyrinth, and can ensure your rights and your children's best interests are safeguarded. But what makes an attorney appropriate for your specific situation? What are the signs that say, "Yes, this is the one!"?

Three are several qualities to consider when hiring a lawyer, so let's break them down:

1. **Specialization in family law**—This is the first and foremost thing to look for. You wouldn't go to a cardiologist for a broken bone, would you? Similarly, you need a lawyer who specializes in family law, which is a unique beast in the legal jungle. Family law attorneys have spent years gaining an understanding of the dynamics of family-related issues, custody battles, and child support regulations. They're well versed in the statutes, legal terminology, and paperwork involved, ensuring that you have the right arsenal to face your high-conflict co-parenting situation.
2. **Experience with high-conflict cases**—You're not just looking for a family law attorney; you're looking for a family law attorney with experience in high-conflict cases. These attorneys have been in the trenches before. They've seen the worst of it and learnt how to work in such environment. Their experience in dealing with intense situations can prove invaluable when it comes to understanding your unique circumstances.
3. **Strong communication skills**—This is a journey you and your attorney will be taking together. You'll need to communicate—a lot. Thus, your attorney should be able to explain complex legal terms in a way you can easily understand. Moreover, they should be able to listen and comprehend your concerns and objectives effectively. The last thing you need in this stressful situation is miscommunication.
4. **Approachability and compassion**—In the grand scheme of things, this may seem like a minor point. But—let me

assure you—it's not. You need someone who is approachable, someone who doesn't make you feel like you're just another case number. They should empathize with your situation, offer comfort during your moments of anxiety, and celebrate small victories with you.

5. **Respectability and connections**—Look for an attorney who has a strong reputation and good relationships within the legal community. They should be known for their ethics, competence, and professionalism. An attorney with a strong network may be able to bring in other professionals to support your case, such as child welfare experts, psychologists, or financial advisers.
6. **Good track record**—Before you choose an attorney, do your homework. Read reviews, ask for references, and check their disciplinary record. Speak with their past clients if possible, as they can provide valuable insights into the attorney's working style, effectiveness, and communication.
7. **Cost and affordability**—Finally, there's no escaping the financial aspect. Understand the attorney's fee structure and ensure it aligns with your budget. Legal help can be expensive, but remember that high cost doesn't necessarily mean high quality.

There you have it. Just remember, finding the right attorney for your high-conflict co-parenting case isn't just about ticking off boxes on a list. It's about finding someone who fits with you, who understands your situation, and will be able to help you deal with the high-conflict co-parenting situation you've found yourself in.

REMEMBER TO PUT YOUR CHILD FIRST

Dealing with your narcissistic ex on a regular basis is not what you want. You don't want to put up with their selfish ways anymore. You don't want to be disrespected and stressed out by them all the time. You thought you'd left all that behind when you broke up with them, so sometimes, it can feel a bit tiresome that you're still dealing with them.

If it weren't for your children, you wouldn't have to put up with them at all. You could cut off all contact and never see them again. But here you are, trying to make sure you're your children can still have a relationship with their other parent. You are making your life uncomfortable and exposing yourself to stress purely for them. That is putting your children first. It can be difficult to keep going, but just keep that in mind. Continue to remind yourself why you are putting up with all of the stress and difficulty—for your children.

Remind yourself on a daily basis to think about things from your child's point of view. What is it that they need? You might want them to feel happy and excited to be back at your house, but they may be sad and missing their other parent. Put them first and let them be sad for a bit; it is about their needs over yours. Likewise, "If they're not upset when you expect them to be, then respond to their happiness" (Rudkin, 2019).

However, do remember that just because you are putting your children first, it doesn't mean that you have to put yourself last. You have needs and wants as well, and you will be able to help your children through all the trials and tribulations far more easily if you are looking after yourself as well. Take some time out when you need it. Indulge your own desires once in a while.

Of course, you aren't going to follow your childhood dream of traveling around the world or buy a brand-new Ferrari. But you can do a workout or have an evening out occasionally. It doesn't make you selfish—it just recharges your batteries so that you have the resources you need to keep showing up for your children.

HELPING YOUR CHILD ADJUST THROUGH IT ALL

Chapter Four covered a lot about how to help your child adjust to divorce. The focus there was on how to help them in the initial stages of the breakup, but obviously, your child will need continued support long after the dust has settled.

Much of the advice about the breakup will continue to apply. Stick to their routines, keep them out of arguments, and give them plenty of space and time to express their emotions. But is there anything else you can do to help them adjust to the reality of living in two homes and to help them with any further changes?

Practicalities

You might be busy worrying about your child's emotional development and well-being, but your child might well be worrying about more mundane considerations. Think about the practicalities of having two homes or, rather, the impracticalities. Even in one home, it's hard enough trying to make sure that there are enough clothes washed, that they have all the uniform and school equipment needed, and that their homework is done on time. But what if you have two homes? How are you going to make sure that they have what they need when they need it? If you are dropping the children off at school and your ex is picking them up, how will you get stuff over to them if you need to?

What if your child is a collector? Where will they keep their collection? At one house, or split between two? What if your child has a special teddy? How will you make sure they have it with them each night? How will you decide on their allowance? Will they get one in each house? Or one to spend between both?

You can really help your child to adjust to two different homes if you iron out some of these small details; they may not seem so important to you, but these are the things that your child will be worrying about because these are the things that affect their daily lives.

Mindset

Help your child see the positives in their situation. Yes, they now have two homes, and they don't get to spend time with both parents at the same time. But there are advantages, too! They get two Christmases, two birthday celebrations, and possibly even two holidays. So they can't have all their things in one place, but they do get two rooms, which gives them the freedom to decorate them differently. In one family I spoke to, Dad was highly allergic to fur, meaning they had never been able to have a pet. After the breakup, the children were able to have a dog at their Mom's house. There are always positives; just look for them together.

Major changes

Be sure to go slow with any major changes, such as moving house. You'll probably be excited about a new place, but remember that your children will be very accustomed and attached to the old one. Go easy on them. Don't just present it to them on the day you are moving in without any warning. Explain to them why you need to move house and, if possible, get their input on what kind of place you would like to live in. Take them along to see some potential places and ask them what they would like their new bedroom to look like. Give them plenty of time to get used to the idea of moving and time to prepare themselves for leaving their own place behind.

The same principle goes for introducing new partners. It's great that you have moved on with your life, and of course, you will be excited about introducing your new partner to your children. But it's probably not a good idea to introduce them as your new partner and move them in a week later. Give them plenty of time to adjust. Perhaps, introduce your partner as a good friend and on neutral ground, such as at the park. Let your children get used to them as a person first before you let them know how important that person is to you. This also gives you a buffer in case your new relationship doesn't work out the way you had planned.

Fun

Of course, your children need reassurance and routine. They need to know that you love them and will be there for them. They need someone who will listen to them and give them space to express their emotions. But don't forget to also have fun. Just as exercise, reading, or gardening lets you take your mind off all the emotions flying around, fun will do the same for your children. Play games, watch movies, bake cookies, ride bikes. Whatever your children enjoy doing. They are children, after all. Not only will it distract them from any anxieties they are feeling, but it will also deliver a healthy dose of normality and will help cement your home as somewhere they can relax and enjoy themselves.

GOING NO CONTACT

The no-contact rule means exactly what it sounds like—no contact whatsoever with the other parent. This isn't just cutting them off your weekend barbecue invite list—it means no calls, no texts, no emails. Nothing. Now, this isn't a tactic employed because you had a disagreement over who the children's dentist should be. This is a strategy used in extreme situations where maintaining contact with the other parent is harmful to you or the children.

Obviously, dealing with a narcissistic ex who makes your life difficult on a daily basis is likely going to have an effect on your mental health. It probably would be much easier on you if you had full custody and your children never saw or spoke to their other parent at all. However, experts agree that in most cases, having a relationship with both biological parents is better for children than losing their relationship with one of them (Fabricius & Luecken, 2007). Studies have also shown that it is better for them to have at least 35% of their time (around 2.5 days per week) with both parents (Nielsen, 2013). This is because children may not fully understand the complexity and nuances of adult issues. The effect on children will vary depending on their age, understanding, and relationship with the other parent. They might feel abandoned, confused, or guilty. Thus, complete no contact could cause confusion, anger, and grief in the short term and could result in many other emotional issues and relationship problems in the future.

Perhaps your ex is beautifully cooperative when it comes to the parenting plan, but they may nonetheless be having an effect on the mental health of your children. Again, get help. Document all your concerns and consult a family therapist or social worker. They will be able to assess the situation and offer advice on preventing further damage; this may well include taking legal action to reduce the amount of time they spend with their other parent or enforcing supervised visitations.

Clearly, if your children are being abused, you will have no choice but to remove them from any contact with your ex. The physical and emotional well-being of your children is paramount. If there is any evidence that they are being harmed in any way, you must immediately report this to the police and social services. In such circumstances, suing for full custody may well be your only option.

In all other circumstances, tread lightly with no contact. It should be used as a last resort where no other interventions have worked, and you have done everything in your power to make the situation work.

If you have followed all the advice in this book, parallel parenting should be working for you. With very little communication and a very structured parenting plan, your ex should have minimal opportunities to manipulate you or cause issues. If they are still not playing by the rules and refuse to follow the measures set out in your agreement, you do have the option to get help. Take all of your documentation to your attorney and get some legal advice on what the law can do to persuade your ex to toe the line. It is critical to involve professionals like lawyers and your therapist when deciding to go no contact.

They can provide guidance and ensure the decision is legally sound.

Implementing the no-contact rule is like attempting to quit sugar cold turkey while working in a candy shop—it's tough, and temptation is everywhere. The challenges can be relentless. You might face legal hurdles, backlash from the other parent, or even your own feelings of guilt and confusion. The other parent might bombard you with messages, bait you into conflicts, or even involve the children. You may even be tempted to respond just this once, but remember, the no-contact rule is like a chain—it's only as strong as its weakest link. Open communication with your children is key during this time. Depending on their age and maturity, explain the situation in a way they can understand. Assure them they're loved and that the decision is not their fault.

The no-contact rule is a big step, and it's not for everyone. But when co-parenting becomes a high-conflict, high-stress scenario, it's a tool in your arsenal. It's not about punishing the other parent; it's about protecting you and your children. Remember, the ultimate goal is always the well-being of your children. You're doing your best, and that's enough.

SUMMARY

Don't let despair set in if your narcissistic ex continues to challenge the waters. Remember, Rome wasn't built in a day. It might take some time for things to calm down and for your ex to realize they can no longer engage their old tactics of manipulation and control. They'll likely push back against your new boundaries to test their durability, but maintain your strength, and in time they'll get the message.

If you're faced with a particularly narcissistic ex, you might find they're attempting to use your children as pawns. It's a tough situation, no doubt, but it's important to resist the urge to retaliate in kind. Avoid getting drawn into an all-out war. Don't engage with them on their level or adopt the mindset of an eye for an eye. Keep a vigilant eye on your children—you know them and their typical behavior. If you see them starting to act out of character and suspect any form of abuse or alienation, reach out to your attorney and/or therapist immediately. Document everything diligently and quietly, as this will be vital evidence if the situation escalates to court. You may also use the documentation in other circumstances—when dealing with social services, police, or your narcissistic ex.

During this trying period, remain calm, focused, and committed to being the best parent you can be. Keep your children's well-being as your foremost priority. Create a safe and nonjudgmental environment for them. Assist them in adjusting to the new circumstances by ensuring all practical aspects of their two homes are covered. Simple things like ensuring they have the right school equipment at the correct home can alleviate their stress. Encourage them to see the positives in this new arrangement and take a slow and steady approach when introducing major changes.

Give serious thought before deciding to go no contact and severing your children's connection with their other parent. As appealing as the idea might seem, in most situations, it's beneficial for children to maintain contact with both parents. However, if there's evidence of abuse, stopping contact might be the only course of action. If not, strive to make it work. Stick to the parallel parenting plan, apply the advice outlined in this book, and aim for a scenario that, while not perfect, is at least manageable.

Action items

- Maintain a watchful eye over your children, and should you notice any signs of manipulation or abuse, seek professional help immediately.
- Vigilantly document your interactions and your children's behavior. This evidence might be crucial in court or when dealing with social services, especially in high-conflict situations.
- Hold firm and continue to assert your boundaries. Resist the urge to retaliate or engage in conflict. Over time, your ex will come to understand that the old ways of manipulation and control no longer work.
- Amidst the chaos, always keep your children's well-being at the forefront. Strive to create a safe, nurturing, and nonjudgmental environment. Ensure that their practical needs are met across both homes, guide them gently through this new arrangement, and introduce changes slowly, focusing on the positive aspects.
- Consider no contact carefully. It is not a decision to be taken lightly. In the absence of abuse, it's generally beneficial for children to maintain a relationship with both parents. Try to make parallel parenting work by sticking to your plan and using the strategies outlined in this guide. Aim for a situation that, while not perfect, is at least manageable.

CONCLUSION

A "conclusion" might seem like an odd way to end this book. We're finishing our time together, but your journey—well, it's just getting started. I won't sugarcoat it; you've got a path ahead of you. But my hope is that you're leaving this book feeling a bit more prepared, a touch more confident, and certainly more optimistic about the journey ahead.

After all, you've endured with your ex, it's finally your moment to reign in your own kingdom. You set the rules. You call the shots. You've got the opportunity to shape your family the way you've always wanted. Yet, your ex, now outside the kingdom's walls, might not take too kindly to this new order of things. They could employ all sorts of strategies to undermine your authority, regain control, or provoke conflict. Your job? Make sure your boundaries are as sturdy as castle walls. Keep them from infiltrating your defenses. But remember, if you spend all your energy guarding the walls, you might miss what is going on inside them. Your children are under your care, and it's your job to ensure they flourish, not just survive.

So, where should you begin?

Firstly, give yourself some time to take stock of your situation. Understand your ex's true nature and level of narcissism. Evaluate your mental state. Perhaps some self-reflection is in order? Building resilience is crucial if you want to co-parent successfully with a difficult ex. Face your own challenges, tackle the negative mindset, and address unhealthy behaviors. Chapters One and Five offer some great strategies to help you come from a place of strength.

Chapter Two discussed constructive ways to respond appropriately. Cease fighting with your ex, particularly in front of your children. Use the grey rock technique of minimal responses and avoid getting riled up. Limit contact as much as possible, communicating only about matters concerning the children. Opt for written communication, which minimizes manipulation opportunities and provides a documented record.

Secondly, examine your relationship with your children. Refer to Chapter Four—are you doing everything possible to help them adjust? Are you a good role model? Consider ways to promote empathy, critical thinking, and self-care. Prioritize open communication, showing your children they can always rely on you as their stable, sensible parent.

Thirdly, construct a comprehensive parenting plan. This document will be the blueprint of your co-parenting arrangement, so ensure you include every tiny detail. Evaluate your communication with your ex. If arguments are still frequent, or if manipulation and control persist, it's time to redefine your interaction strategy. Chapter Seven provides insights on what to include in your plan and how to go about it. Make sure the plan is legally binding, with both of your signatures.

Lastly, don't go on this journey solo. Everyone needs a support network. Surround yourself and your children with positive influences. Consider therapy if you need help addressing certain issues. Seek legal assistance if the relationship with your ex worsens.

As I bid you farewell, think of Glinda in *The Wizard of Oz*, pointing you towards the beginning of the Yellow Brick Road. Remember Dorothy and her companions' discoveries along their journey: wisdom, heart, and courage. Likewise, equip yourself with knowledge, take care of your children (and yourself), and face everything bravely. If you can manage that, you're well on your way to creating the nurturing home environment you desire for yourself and your children.

BIBLIOGRAPHY

Ainsworth, M. D. S., Blehar, M. C., Waters, E., & Wall, S. (1978). *Patterns of attachment: A psychological study of the strange situation.* Lawrence Erlbaum Associates.

Amato, P. R. (2001). Children of divorce in the 1990s: An update of the Amato and Keith (1991) meta-analysis. *Journal of Family Psychology, 15*(3), 355–370.

Amato, P. R., & Sobolewski, J. M. (2001). The effects of divorce and marital discord on adult children's psychological well-being. *American Sociological Review, 66*(6), 900–921.

American Academy of Pediatrics. (2016). Media and Young Minds. Pediatrics, 138(5). https://doi.org/10.1542/peds.2016-2591

American Psychiatric Association. (2013). *Diagnostic and statistical manual of mental disorders* (5th ed.). American Psychiatric Publishing.

Brummelman, E., Thomaes, S., Nelemans, S. A., Orobio de Castro, B., Overbeek, G., & Bushman, B. J. (2015). Origins of narcissism in children. *Proceedings of the National Academy of Sciences, 112*(12), 3659–3662. https://doi.org/10.1073/pnas.1420870112

Durvasula R. (2017). *Should I stay or should I go: Surviving a relationship with a narcissist*. Post Hill Press.

Dwyer, C. P., Hogan, M. J., & Stewart, I. (2014). An integrated critical thinking framework for the 21st century. *Thinking Skills and Creativity, 12,* 43–52. https://doi.org/10.1016/j.tsc.2013.12.004

Fabricius W. V., & Luecken L. J. (2007). Postdivorce living arrangements, parent conflict, and long-term physical health correlates for children of divorce. *Journal of Family Psychology, 21*(2), 195–205. https://doi.org/10.1037/0893-3200.21.2.195

Fleming, V. (Director). (1939). *The wizard of Oz* [Film]. Metro-Goldwyn-Mayer.

Hammond, C. (2019, August 16). *How to counteract parental alienation.* Psych Central. https://psychcentral.com/pro/exhausted-woman/2019/08/how-to-counteract-parental-alienation

Hammons, A. J., & Fiese, B. H. (2011). Is frequency of shared family meals related to the nutritional health of children and adolescents? *Pediatrics, 127*(6), e1565–e1574.

Kendler, K. S., Aggen, S. H., Czajkowski, N., Røysamb, E., Tambs, K., Torgersen, S., Neale, M. C., & Reichborn-Kjennerud, T. (2008). The structure of genetic and environmental risk factors for DSM-IV personality disorders: A multivariate twin study. *Archives of General Psychiatry, 65*(12), 1438–1446. https://doi.org/10.1001/archpsyc.65.12.1438

Livesley, W. J., Jang, K. L., & Vernon, P. A. (2018). The genetic and environmental basis of the relationship between narcissism and the broad dimensions of personality. *Journal of Affective Disorders, 238*, 410–417.

Lo, I. (2022, May 3). Narcissistic parent abuse — 5 types of invisible narcissistic abuse. *Eggshell Therapy and Coaching*. https://eggshelltherapy.com/narcissistic-parent-abuse/

Luo, Y. L., Cai, H., & Song, H. (2014). A behavioral genetic study of intrapersonal and interpersonal dimensions of narcissism. *PLoS ONE, 9*(4), e93403. https://doi.org/10.1371/journal.pone.0093403

Mehrabian, A. (1971). *Silent messages*. Wadsworth.

Mehrabian, A., & Wiener, M. (1967). Decoding of inconsistent communications. *Journal of Personality and Social Psychology, 6*(1), 109–114.

Mischel, W., Shoda, Y., & Rodriguez, M. L. (1989). Delay of gratification in children. *Science, 244*(4907), 933–938. https://doi.org/10.1126/science.2658056

Neff, K. D. (2011). *Self-compassion: Stop beating yourself up and leave insecurity behind*. Harper Collins.

Nielsen, L. (2013). Shared residential custody: Review of the research (Part I of II). *American Journal of Family Law, 27*(1), 61–71.

Rideout, V. J., Foehr, U. G., & Roberts, D. F. (2010). *Generation M2: Media in the lives of 8- to 18-year-olds*. Henry J. Kaiser Family Foundation.

Rudkin, A. (2019, July 11). What does it mean to put your children first? *Only-Mums*. https://www.onlymums.org/information/what-does-it-mean-to-put-your-children-first

Seligman, M. E. (2002). *Authentic happiness: Using the new positive psychology to realize your potential for lasting fulfillment*. Free Press.

Southwick, S. M., & Charney, D. S. (2012). *Resilience: The science of mastering life's greatest challenges*. Cambridge University Press.

Wielgosz, J., Goldberg, S. B., Kral, T. R., Dunne, D. J., & Davidson, R. J. (2019). Mindfulness meditation and psychopathology. *Annual Review of Clinical Psychology, 7*(15), 285–316. https://doi.org/10.1146/annurev-clinpsy-021815-093423

Download your free "Co-Parenting Plan" to ensure the best for you and your children

With this plan, you will:

1- Communicate Effectively

Handle challenging conversations with structure and foster open dialogue, even with your difficult ex-partner

2- Strengthen Boundaries

Establish firm, well-defined boundaries to protect yourself and your children from control and manipulation

3- Ensure the best for your children

Create a stable, nurturing environment for your child or children, regardless of your ex's personality traits.

Go to: *www.lighthousebooks.co/coparentingplan*

Or scan the QR code

ABOUT THE AUTHOR

Michael Marino is an experienced therapist focused on guiding individuals through challenging relationships and promoting healthy child development amidst adversity. Michael combines personal experiences, psychology research, and counseling insights in his books to offer practical advice on co-parenting, relationships, and difficult family transitions. He's dedicated to empowering individuals to heal from past trauma and create fulfilling futures. He currently resides in New York with his wife.